Today's Guide to Greenhouse Gardening

Today's Guide to Greenhouse Gardening

Bob Price

Resident expert on
ATV's *Gardening Today* programme

With a Foreword by
CYRIL FLETCHER

WILLIAM LUSCOMBE

First published in Great Britain by
William Luscombe Publisher Ltd,
The Mitchell Beazley Group,
Artists House, 14–15 Manette Street,
London, W1V 5LB.
1976

Hardback ISBN 0 86002 123 8
Paperback ISBN 0 86002 144 0

Printed in Hong Kong by
Mandarin Publishers Ltd.

Acknowledgments

Many people, organisations and commercial companies have provided valuable advice, help and/or illustrations for this book, and to them all my grateful thanks are due.

In particular I should like to acknowledge the assistance given to me by The Royal Horticultural Society in introducing me to the specialist photographers whose pictures are reproduced in the book. Also, my thanks are especially due to The Orchid Society of Great Britain, some of whose superb plates illustrate Chapter 13.

Finally, and to my great pleasure, my friend and colleague on *Gardening Today*, Cyril Fletcher, has written a Foreword to the book in his own inimitable way. Much appreciated.

BOB PRICE

Contents

Illustrations

Picture credits
The author would like to thank those manufacturers and suppliers of greenhouses, greenhouse plants, accessories and equipment who so kindly loaned the illustrations of their products reproduced in this book.

Grateful thanks are also due to the following for permission to reproduce the photographs indicated:

Colour plates: Floraprint Ltd, Calverton, Nottingham, for Nos. 2 and 3 of Black Hamburgh grapes and *Campsis radicans;* **Mr.** Roy Elliott of Birmingham and The Alpine Garden Society: No. 6; The Orchid Society of Great Britain: Nos. 9, 10, 11, 12, 13; The Shell Photographic Unit: Nos. 14, 15, 16; Pan Britannic Industries Ltd: Nos 17, 18.

Front Cover by Derek Peters
Black and white plates: Roy Elliott: Nos. 7, 8, 9; J. E. Downward: Nos. 10, 26, 28, 30b, 32, 33, 34, 35, 37, 40, 42, 47, 48, 49,

50, 51, 52, 53, 55, 64, 67, 68, 69, 72; Brian Furner: Nos. 16, 57, 58, 59, 60, 61, 62, 63, 65, 66, 90; Thomas Rochford & Sons Ltd: Nos. 22, 23, 24, 29, 31, 36, 39, 43; H. Smith: Nos. 25, 27, 30a, 38, 41, 44, 46, 54, 56, 70, 71, 73, 74, 75, 76; The Orchid Society of Great Britain: Nos. 79, 80, 81, 82; Neville Orchids Ltd, Baltonsborough, Somerset: 83; Shell Photographic Unit: Nos. 84, 85, 86, 87, 88, 89.

Drawings by Annabel Milne

Foreword

by Cyril Fletcher

There is one thing in Great Britain that you can really depend on and that is the weather! 'Depend on it?' you demand in amazement. Yes. You may depend on it as an opening gambit for conversation. You may depend on it being pretty ghastly for long intervals . . . especially on Bank Holidays and in the height of summer. But it is at its most dependable in its determination to be at its very worst when you have set a day aside, a few days aside or even your whole holiday to work in the garden. For this reason alone a greenhouse is an absolute necessity – so that you may further many of your gardening chores in the dry and the warm regardless. Also, a greenhouse will give you a wondrous new world of gardening where exotic plants from all corners of the globe can be coaxed into flower.

Bob and I find, when we do our gardening programmes for ATV *Gardening Today*, that each time we schedule a recording in the greenhouse there is a heat-wave – even in December – but when we are outside in 'blazing June' then there is a blizzard. But we, unlike your good selves, are not our own masters. We have to obey the Producer and the planned positions of the cameramen, the lights, the microphones and what have you.

It is under such conditions as war, a revolution, or making a gardening programme, that one finds the sort of person of whom you can make a friend. These conditions stretch a man. With Bob it doesn't show that he's stretched – he looks roughly the same length always – but you realise that here is dependability (like the weather), here is a fund of knowledge which is so firmly based that no crisis will allow him to forget or falter. He is a man of stirling worth who knows his job. But one of the best things about Bob Price is that he is such good company. You will find ample proof of this in his book. He will share his knowledge with you pleasantly and with charm. As you learn from him you will be in good company. Here is your chance to get to know him now. I have known and worked closely with him for over two years and enjoyed every minute of our work together.

CYRIL FLETCHER

1 Why do you want a greenhouse?

Ardent gardening fanatics would give you a hundred answers to this question – in fact, with them the question does not even arise. They would say it was an essential part of their gardening routine.

This to a large extent is true, but let's take it that you are still at the stage of considering the pros and cons.

As we shall see in the next chapter, greenhouses come in a variety of sizes, shapes and styles, so a careful selection can ensure that yours need not be an eyesore.

If heated (and even if not, although to a lesser extent) it can be a haven where your gardening interests are utilised and exploited even in the dead of winter, and if family problems get you down you can always retire to your glasshouse den! You'll be pleasantly surprised, too, how fascinating you'll find it to experiment and 'play around' with the propagation and growing of plants, and how wonderfully satisfying your first real success will be.

Keeping the house stocked with flowering and foliage plants is an expensive luxury if, as they begin to deteriorate, you throw them out and buy new ones. How much less expensive and far more satisfying it would be to propagate your own house plants in the greenhouse, grow them on until they are at their best and then take them into the house. These would replace the plants in the house which are beginning to look jaded and which would be taken to the greenhouse to be trimmed up and nursed back to health. This cycling of plants between house and greenhouse can go on almost indefinitely, with just an occasional new variety being introduced as the fancy takes you – and you will be surprised how rewarding this little side of greenhouse life can be.

Have you ever thought of the joy of picking ripe strawberries in early May, keeping a supply of fresh lettuce throughout the winter, cutting fresh mint at Christmas, forcing rhubarb or growing mushrooms under the staging? All these and many more can be yours with a heated greenhouse.

Even without heat you can grow tomatoes successfully or fill your greenhouse with the luxury of a grape vine, and if you have a 'lean-to' facing south or south-west, there's nothing to stop you growing a fan-trained peach, nectarine or apricot on the wall.

All right, so the purchase and heating of a greenhouse can be expensive – so can a fortnight's holiday in Majorca – but as with the holiday you must consider the cost in relation to the return benefits you derive – benefits of pleasure, satisfaction, peace of mind and even, of course, finance. Gardening is a great subject for social intercourse, and if you are a successful greenhouse gardener you will always have something to talk about.

So far we have mainly discussed the pros, but there is one con you must seriously weigh up before you decide. That is the fact that a greenhouse does demand some of your time – at least three visits a week in winter (if it is heated) and daily during the spring, summer and autumn. This may sound a lot, but visits need not be of long duration, often just a few minutes to make sure that everything is all right – and anyway, as you become interested and results begin to show, you will even find yourself hurrying home just to get into that greenhouse! Controlled automation (heating, ventilating and watering) in the greenhouse will save you a lot of time there, but we'll say more about that in Chapter 6.

2 What type of greenhouse do you require?

First of all you must decide just what you most want to undertake in your greenhouse – indoor plants, vegetables, fruit, perhaps propagation, or even a combination of all these things. Then there is the siting to bear in mind; obviously if the only space you have available is against a house wall there will be no alternative but to choose a lean-to, but if you incorporate a greenhouse in your original garden design, your choice would be so much wider. Finally, there is the conservatory type for the gardener (or just plant lover) who wants to make a glassed extension to his house, normally with access only from the house itself.

Of course initial cost is important – it can be the most important item for consideration – but do remember that with few exceptions you get just what you pay for. An apparently inexpensive greenhouse can be a cheap one in every respect – difficult to erect, with ill-fitting doors and vents, and other faults all making you wish that you had saved that little bit longer for a better one.

Having decided we really do want a greenhouse, let us consider the main types there are to choose from:

1. *The traditional span or ridge greenhouse.*
2. *The lean-to greenhouse, and threequarter span.*
3. *The semi-spherical or solardome type.*
4. *The porch, conservatory or verandah.*
5. *Dutch lights.*
6. *Polythene or PVC in lieu of glass.*

The size of your selected type will probably be governed by space and site available and/or initial cost. If neither of these two reasons impose any restrictions, then I would start with a greenhouse about 12 ft × 8 ft, which is not too large to heat but large enough to allow plenty of room in which to work. With a 2 ft wide paved path along the centre from door to end, it will still give you 3 ft of growing space either side. Guttering to catch rain-water is an important item, and I would suggest that the downpipe from the guttering be curved through the side into a water tank inside the greenhouse itself. In this way you will always have available for your plants

rain-water at greenhouse temperature, which, as it contains health-giving minerals etc. is far better than tap-water, which is often at anything but the temperature in which the plants are standing. Don't forget, by the way, to put an overflow pipe from your tank to an underground rubble-filled soakaway or you could have trouble in heavy rains.

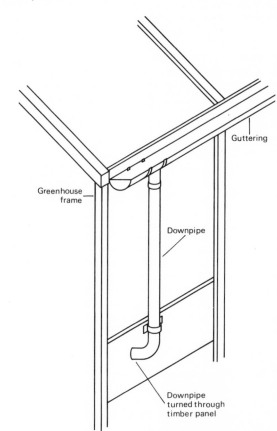

Guttering

Greenhouse frame

Downpipe

Downpipe turned through timber panel

Below left. Fig. 1 PVC downpipe turned into side
of greenhouse through timber panel to feed
rain-water container inside

Below Plate 1 AGL aluminium span greenhouse

I would also consider, in addition to normal vents, a
louvred panel low down in the door and one high up
in the gable end of the greenhouse. These could be
adjustable, but they would allow air to circulate from
low down to high up even in winter when the normal
vents have to be kept closed, thus utilising the simple
scientific fact that hot air rises. Louvred panels also
allow air access whilst restricting actual draughts as
much as possible. All plants hate draughts.

1. *The traditional span or ridge greenhouse,* with side walls of
brick, timber or concrete would still be my first choice
for general horticultural use. Its square or rectangular
shape enables it to fit easily into any garden design, it will
allow for the absolute maximum of staging space
(under which you can store pots, tools etc. besides

growing mushrooms, chicory, rhubarb, etc.) and the
solid walls help it to maintain heat more effectively,
even in winter. Many people ask how a rectangular
greenhouse should be aligned lengthways, and although
the old traditional siting was north-south I would say
it could be just as effective east-west or on any alignment
it falls in your garden design. After all, it is glass all
round and you can organise your plant growing and
propagation according to the sun and the side of your
greenhouse it falls on for the longest period each day.
To save money by conserving winter heat, always try
and site your greenhouse where it will be protected
from the cold north and east winds. The glass-to-ground
aluminium span greenhouse, as illustrated, is strong,
has a great diversity of uses, and is still comparatively
inexpensive. The vertical sides are a space-saving feature.

A new race of traditional span greenhouses has recently
sprung up, not revolutionary in design but based on the
fact that there's hardly any difference between ordinary
gardeners and commercial growers. In other words,
certain manufacturers' principles have changed from
quantity to quality. So these aluminium alloy amateurs'
greenhouses (you notice I never call them glasshouses – I
spent six war years in the Army!) are built just as strongly,
just as draught-proof, in fact with just as few imper-
fections as any commercial house. I recently received
one in kit form from the makers and, believe it or not,
it took two of us just four hours to erect the framework –
the glass followed later – and the only tools we used
were a screw-driver and a spanner. This particular type
of greenhouse is so strong that it needs no concrete
foundations or brick base. You don't even require
perfectly level ground, just sink the sides where necessary
a few inches into the soil and anchor them with simple
ground anchor cleats. The clear and concise assembly
instructions suggest that you start by selecting and laying
out in precise formation the various component parts,
and consequent erection is easy. Integral guttering with
plastic end-stops and outlets are part of the basic greenhouse framework, and non-perishable draught-excluders
are fitted to the suspended sliding door. With the patented
glazing system, the glass is gently but firmly pressed
against gaskets set in a strong rigid glazing bar. Cover
caps are ready drilled and the holes can't let water in.

I would still like a couple of louvred panels in the end
walls to assist with air circulation in warm weather,
but the basic strength, precision and design of this type
of greenhouse must give them a great future.

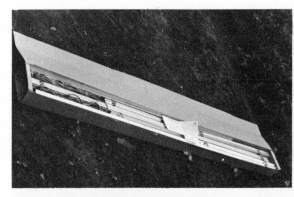

Of course the most popular type of ridge or span greenhouse being purchased at the present time is that which is constructed simply and completely with aluminium, stainless steel and glass; with glass to ground on vertical sides. They are easy to erect, will not warp, rust, discolour, decay or even need painting – in fact, with having stainless steel clips, they are virtually maintenance free. If the Garden of Eden had sported such a greenhouse, the serpent would probably be walking on tip toes now!

2. *The lean-to* is, as its name suggests, half a span greenhouse built to lean against a wall. For the beginner it is always best to site this facing south or south-west, although for some specialist growers of ferns etc. a

Plate 3   12ft × 8ft Edenlite greenhouse

north-facing aspect would be all right. You notice I never mention an eastward-facing aspect as some plants hate to have the warm sun on their leaves in the early morning, and in any case the cold east winds in winter would increase the difficulty of maintaining a reasonably high temperature. To this end, of course, the warm wall of the house must help, and it is against this wall that successfully may be grown peaches, apricots, nectarines, passion flowers or even geraniums. One other advantage of a lean-to greenhouse is that it is so easily accessible from the house, often being sited alongside the kitchen door. If you mainly want to grow tomatoes, chrysanthemums etc. in the ground-level soil in the greenhouse then your lean-to will want to have the glass right down to the ground, but if you prefer to grow plants

on the staging then you will have timber, brick or concrete walls up to the staging level. Don't forget to make sure that the greenhouse bricks match those of the house.

The threequarter span is a lean-to with an additional short span which anchors to the top of a wall. It offers greater space and is a better sun-trap than the ordinary lean-to, and consequently is more efficient in some ways. It is also much more expensive, and therefore very rarely manufactured these days; in fact I am only really mentioning it as being of technical interest.

The high-south-wall-greenhouse is a more modern type designed, as its name suggests, with its highest side

Plate 4   10ft × 8ft Westdock high-south-wall greenhouse

facing the midday sun, i.e. the south. The most critical period for the trapping of solar radiation is in the winter when the sun's elevation is at its lowest and your fuel bills are at their highest. It has one side higher than the other and a single pitch roof. The high wall is sited to face south and is angled to trap solar radiation from the low-elevated winter sun. Other features include adjustable louvred ventilators, an effective cushioned glazing system, built-in bench supports, and strong and rigid construction. Of course there is still room for improvement, but I think this is a bold design with a touch of the future about it. We must accept the fact that solar radiation is one of the most powerful of natural forces, and much more thought should be given to the harnessing of it. Harnessed and stored solar energy is already widely used to heat swimming pools etc. This greenhouse is designed to trap solar energy; the next step should be to store it and release it as it is required.

3. *The semi-spherical type of greenhouse*, sometimes called the solardome for obvious reasons, is only just beginning to make an impact on the gardening public. This type eliminates the problems we mentioned above of directional siting, and its shape gives great strength and maximum sunshine hours. It is normally constructed of metal and glass so that maintenance costs are minimal, but if you are considering this type make sure that you utilise in the best way possible the space and shape you have available. You see, the walls all slope inwards so the plants you grow near to them will have to be low-growing, with the taller plants towards the centre.

Outside and central circular stagings are usually available with this type, which I think will become more popular as time goes on.

4. *The porch, conservatory or verandah* types of plant houses are normally built with, or just added on to, the house as required. Their obvious advantages are accessibility and heating, but as there are usually two doors (one to the house and one to outside) a great disadvantage from the plants' point of view is draught. This problem must be watched carefully if you do not want to lose some of your choice plants. If you find you could perhaps build a

21

Plate 6 Conservatory by Richardson of Darlington

porch, conservatory or verandah yourself, I would certainly consult first of all an architect and a landscape architect to advise you on blending with the house design and making proper provision for the growing of your plants. If there has to be two doors, perhaps one need not be sited directly opposite the other, and so on.

5. *Dutch lights* are large sheets of glass (sometimes almost 60 in. × 30 in.) held in light wooden frameworks. Although they were originally intended for use only in garden frames, complete greenhouses with glass to

ground are now made of them. This makes them ideal for growing crops in the ground-level greenhouse soil, to allow maximum height for growth. Tomatoes, chrysanthemums, carnations, vegetables, vines etc. can all be grown successfully in this way. Of course, staging can also be erected in Dutch light greenhouses, but with so much glass the cost of maintaining a reasonable growing temperature throughout the winter must be greater than for the solid-wall greenhouses. They are also subject to sharp fluctuations of temperature even in summer, and this is a point which must be guarded

23

against. Remember an all-glass-sided greenhouse leaves everything in view from outside, and unless the area underneath the staging is kept tidy, boxes, pots, tools etc. can become an eyesore.

In their favour, Dutch light greenhouses have the advantages of, as we have said, admitting maximum sunlight and sometimes being cheaper to buy than the traditional types.

6. Although, with photosynthesis in mind, clear glass is far better, we are hearing a lot these days about the use of plastics in the construction of greenhouses, or 'tunnels' as they are sometimes called. Polyethylene, better known as polythene, is translucent, but needs to be renewed at fairly frequent intervals since continued bright sunlight seems to affect it. Heavy duty polythene is often stretched over a series of semi-circular metal rods to form what is known commercially as a 'tunnel', and this is used extensively to protect young shrubs and other plants through the winter.

Polyvinyl-chloride or PVC is another form of plastic sheeting which is transparent but far less flexible than polythene. Affixed to a timber framework, PVC can make a comparatively inexpensive greenhouse, but don't expect the same results as you would get with a traditional glass one. Accumulated dirt is much more difficult to remove from plastic than from glass, and as this results in the quality of light transmitted being greatly reduced, there is no doubt that plastic-covered greenhouses can only be regarded as temporary units which require renewing from time to time. We must admit, though, that plastic does give one ample protection from draughts, rain and wind, and is excellent for providing an inner lining to a glass greenhouse to help conserve heat and maintain a higher temperature in winter.

There is also the combined shed and greenhouse for the gardener whose space is limited, half the shed being used for the storage of tools and for potting.

When erecting your greenhouse do make sure that first of all you lay an adequate concrete, brick or concrete block foundation, the top surface of which is perfectly level all round. Even with bricks or blocks it is better to lay them on a concrete foundation, and to use a spirit level for the top surface. (To make the concrete, thoroughly mix together 4 parts gravel, 2 parts sand and 1 part cement all measured by bulk,

and well water to a consistency which is something like thick porridge.) If the foundations are not level, you will find that the sections of your greenhouse don't fit as perfectly as they should – and it won't be the manufacturer's fault, it will be yours.

Make sure you have a dry paved access path from the house to and through the greenhouse, laid with a 2 in. thick concrete paving bedded on cement mortar. The position of the greenhouse, whether it be near to or far from the house, should be carefully selected by you so as to be both pleasing and practical.

One other point – whichever type of greenhouse you choose, pay particular attention to the number of vents and consequent air circulation. If there are too many vents, some can be kept closed, but if the air is too stuffy you can't open a vent which isn't there! Remember good air circulation (not draughts) is a very important factor where plant health is concerned. One of the main contributory factors to the diseases botrytis and mildew is poor circulation of air.

Of course there will always be the argument as to which framework medium to use, metal or wood. The general appearance of a greenhouse must play an important part in its selection, especially in smaller gardens where it is in full view from the house. With the thought of it blending in with its natural surroundings, there is no doubt that cedar wood is very attractive, provided it is treated regularly with a suitable proprietary preservative. Teak and Oak are also very durable timbers, but more costly than western red cedar. White wood timbers are nothing like as durable, and need annual applications of white lead paint to preserve the wood and reflect the light. Of course, to the handyman timber has the advantage of being easier to work with as far as alterations and additions are concerned.

Almost all metal greenhouses these days are constructed with an aluminium alloy, which is strong, durable and needs very little maintenance. The glazing bars are usually narrower than the timber ones, and consequently less light is impeded. With the increasing world-wide price of timber the cost difference is now very little, but there is no doubt which will last the longer.

However, if well manufactured, both metal and timber-framed greenhouses can be very efficient, but you are the one who will have to look at what you select, maintain it and work in it, so, after all, the choice is yours.

3 Heated or unheated?

The range of plants, flowers, fruits and vegetables which can be grown in a greenhouse depends almost wholly on the minimum temperature that can be maintained in the winter.

1. Unheated greenhouses

Maybe your resources were stretched when you purchased your greenhouse, and although you want to install an efficient heating system, it may take a year or so before you feel you can spare the extra capital. On the other hand, your greenhouse may be unheated from choice, but either way you can get lots of pleasure and satisfaction if you never lose sight of its limitations.

I used to keep a Simplex Propagator with a plastic cover and thermostatically-controlled soil warming cable in an unheated greenhouse, and in this I was able to germinate seeds and root tender cuttings successfully from early April onwards. I would sow tomato seeds so that the young plants would be ready to plant out in the greenhouse by mid-May, and of course would get a satisfactory crop each year.

Contrary to popular belief, excellent crops of grapes can be produced from a vine planted in an unheated greenhouse, and of course, cucumbers and melons can be grown, too, if not started too early.

I am very fond of alpines or rock plants, and I always keep a selection of these in my unheated greenhouse, grown in suitable gritty composts in 6 in. or 8 in. diameter half pots. I say 'gritty' because alpines do insist on good drainage – they won't sit with their feet in water – but the rest of the compost would depend upon the individual tastes of the various plants, alkaline, acid, loamy, light, etc. A few of the plants I enjoy growing in this way include:

Androsace in variety
Kabschia Saxifrages in variety
Ramonda pyrenaica
Lewisia in variety
Rhodohypoxis baurei

Campanula zoysii
Gentiana acaulis
Fuchsia Tom Thumb
Jeffersonia dubia
Verbena chamaedrifolia
Sedum Capa Blanca etc. etc.

An attractive display may be had in an unheated greenhouse by growing hardy and half-hardy shrubs and plants in pots. Not only will these come into flower a little earlier than outside, but they will not be spoilt in any way by wind or rain.

Plate 7   *Jeffersonia dubia*

Plate 8 Kabschia saxifrage 'Valerie Finnis'

Of the shrubs you can try, the exotic yet fairly easy-to-grow camellia is the first which comes to mind. This was sometimes considered to be tender, mainly because early flowers were often damaged by late frosts, but if planted outside in lime-free moist soil containing plenty of humus in a situation where they are protected from the morning sun, camellias are now found to be perfectly hardy and most prolific.

However, for a cold greenhouse display, plant your young camellia in a suitably-sized pot containing a mixture of equal parts by bulk of grit, loam and peat or leafmould, and only water with rain-water at greenhouse temperature. (Remember, by the way, not to wet the leaves whilst the morning sun is on them.) *Hydrangea hortensis* and its many varieties are other shrubs which revel in cold greenhouse conditions, and will produce

Plate 9   *Ramonda pyrenaica*

their huge flowers quite a few weeks earlier than outside. Don't forget to use one of the proprietary hydrangea colourants to intensify the colour of the flowers.

Another shrub which shows its appreciation of the protection of the unheated greenhouse by producing earlier and better double pink flowers than outside is *Prunus triloba* 'flore pleno'. The syringa (lilac), dwarfish *Rhododendron praecox*, winter-flowering heathers (*Erica carnea*), Chinese witch hazel (*Hamamelis mollis*); and many others can all be successfully grown and flowered in a cold greenhouse.

For a colourful spring display, why not lift in the autumn, pot and bring into the unheated greenhouse such herbaceous plants as astilbes, polyanthus, forget-me-nots, dicentras (Bleeding Heart), lily-of-the-valley and what I consider the best of them all, the Christmas rose (*Helleborus niger*). Of course there are so many bulbs – from narcissus to iris and so on – to pot up in the autumn for flowering in spring, and for summer flowers in the unheated greenhouse, why not try the lilies such as *L. regale*, *L. auratum*, *L. speciosum* etc. together with gloxinias and begonias.

Plate 10   Well-stocked greenhouse

Fruits such as peaches, nectarines, apricots, vines (try the variety 'Black Hamburgh') have all been mentioned as being suitable to grow in an unheated greenhouse, and lettuce seed sown in October will be ready for cutting the following April. Each autumn I plant a few roots of mint in the cool greenhouse, from which we go on cutting throughout most of the winter.

2. Heated greenhouses – (a) Cool

If a minimum temperature of 10°C (50°F) can be maintained you can call it a 'cool' greenhouse, in which all the things mentioned in connection with the unheated greenhouse can be grown even more successfully plus, of course, many more. (A word of caution here, with shrubs such as camellias and the others, be careful that the temperature is not allowed to shoot up too high in the daytime, as this sometimes causes flower buds to drop off.) Indian azaleas (*Azalea indica*) can be grown in a cool greenhouse. These are the popular evergreen house plants which flower between Christmas and Easter, and should only be watered and sprayed with rain-water at greenhouse temperature, not forgetting

to add some liquid fertiliser about once a fortnight. Remove all dead flowers and stand the plant (with the pot plunged into the soil up to its rim) outside during the summer. In this way *Azalea indica* can be kept for years.

Other plants which a cool greenhouse can accommodate include mimosa (*Acacia dealbata*) with scented fluffy yellow flowers, and climbers such as passion flower (*Passiflora*), the beautiful reddish-purple Bougainvillea, and *Plumbago capensis* with its lovely pale blue flowers. The huge bulbs of hippeastrums, sometimes mistakenly called amaryllis, can be made to produce those strikingly handsome flowers on their thick sturdy stems in a cool greenhouse, and regal pelargoniums, too, although they do not flower until the summer. Indoor winter-flowering primulas such as *P. obconica* and *P. malacoides* grow well in a cool greenhouse, and another good subject is *Cyclamen persicum*, the Persian Cyclamen (was it Cyril who thought the Persian Cyclamen was the Shah's bodyguard?). These last three can all be grown from seed sown the previous summer. Fruit and vegetables as mentioned for an unheated greenhouse can be grown even better where a minimum winter temperature of 10°C (50°F) is maintained, with the added bonus that they can all be started into growth that much earlier.

3. Heated greenhouses – (b) Warm

A warm greenhouse is one where a minimum temperature of 13°C (55°F) can be maintained throughout even the coldest winter days and nights. Your heating bill could be prodigious, but your rewards would be very satisfying in that a great many fascinating tropical or 'stove' plants (in addition to those already mentioned) can be cultivated. The strongly-scented beautiful pure white flowers of both the gardenia and the stephanotis are best brought to perfection in a warm greenhouse.

The poinsettia (*Euphorbia pulcherrima*) with its brilliant scarlet bracts at Christmas is a plant which is grown out of doors in South Africa so that the higher temperature and plenty of sun of its natural habitat is effectively reproduced in a warm greenhouse.

Saintpaulia (African violet), *Begonia rex*, *Brunfelsia calycina* (a purple-flowered evergreen) and many more fascinating house plants need a warm greenhouse.

Finally, a mention of the strawberry 'Royal Sovereign', which can be potted up in late summer in a peaty compost, left outside in a sheltered spot for the root system to become established, and then introduced to warm greenhouse conditions in February. We did this in the ATV Garden greenhouse and picked luscious ripe strawberries in early May.

4 Types of heating

Before you make a move to install a heating system you should give careful thought not only to its initial cost but also to how much it will cost each year to maintain the desired minimum winter temperature. As a rough guide, to heat a greenhouse to a minimum temperature of 10°C (50°F) will cost about twice as much as the same one heated to 7°C (45°F).

1. Electricity

There is, of course, always the fact of available time to look after your greenhouse heating, and if you are away from home a lot then automation in some form or another must be a prime factor. This is where we must mention electricity, which, whilst being more expensive to run than most other methods, is clean, easy, efficient and very labour-saving. A cheaper way to use electricity is to install some form of storage heater, the heat of which is recharged at off-peak periods. Before embarking on this type of heating (storage heaters can lose heat more quickly in a glass-walled greenhouse than a brick-walled house), I would suggest you obtain advice from your local Electricity Authority.

Tubular heating with electrically heated weather-proofed horticultural tubes in lengths from 2 ft to 12 ft

fitted to the greenhouse walls is possibly the least expensive way of heating by electricity taking up very little working space.

I like the electrical fan heaters, which are simple to install and may be fixed or movable. They blow warm air through the house, and this air circulation is beneficial to the health of the plants. In warm weather they can be used to circulate the air without heat, which would therefore be helpful in the successful growing of carnations and chrysanthemums. Most fan heaters have a built-in thermostat, and although not as sensitive as the rod type, they ensure reasonable running costs. A fan heater should be placed near to the door and at least 2 ft away from the side of the greenhouse or other obstructions. Of course, water should not be allowed to drip on it at any time, and make sure that there are no plants in direct line with the actual blow-out of hot air. Some floor-standing fan heaters have specially designed louvres fitted to the inlet and outlet apertures to ensure that the warm or cool air is blown along the ground so that the circulation of air works from ground level upwards. Usually an automatic cut-out protects the element in case the air flow is interrupted. They are probably an improvement on tubular heaters, but, having moving parts, must wear out in time.

Plate 13   Camplex 18 in. rod-type hydraulic soil/air thermostat

Water-filled heaters heated by an electric element are valuable for providing a little humidity as well as heat, and giving an even stable temperature.

To heat a lean-to greenhouse it is sometimes possible to install an extension of the house central heating. This is quite all right if you remember that this is a dry heat and some provision must be made to humidify the atmosphere.

All types of electrical heating should be under thermostatic control, so that once it is switched on and the thermostat set at the required temperature, you can go to the office in a peaceful frame of mind without any worries about climatic temperature variations.

The inexpensive types of thermostat are suitable for loads from 1200 to 2000 watts, and can be regulated to control temperatures between 2°C and 24°C (35°F and 75°F). These are hand-operated models and are usually accurate to within 2°C to 4°C (4°F to 6°F).

The rod types are more expensive but also much more accurate, usually being accurate to about $\frac{3}{4}$°C (1°F). These models are capable of controlling up to 4000 watts, and the temperature control range extends usually from −1°C to 32°C (30°F to 90°F).

Remember that any electrical apparatus is safe only if it is installed by an experienced electrician, and only if the correct types of fittings are employed. A degree of

Plate 14   Shilton gas greenhouse heater

dampness is essential in a greenhouse, so it is vital that waterproof fittings, connections, and cables are used.

Local Electricity Boards are always ready to offer sound practical advice on proposed installations, and while you are in touch ask them for a copy of their current booklet called *Electricity in Your Garden*. It is a useful little booklet which could offer you quite a few very helpful hints.

Before leaving the subject of heating by electricity, don't forget that the supply must be brought from the house or garage, so bear this in mind when siting your greenhouse. I would always advocate taking the supply by underground cable rather than overhead as it is unobtrusive, not unsightly, and (I hope) safely out of harm's way. I say 'I hope' because although underground cable is specially protected against damp and chemical damage, it, and you, could be damaged by a sharp spade or fork. With that in mind, then, I should bury the cable beneath the lawn or pathway.

2. Paraffin

Paraffin stoves are much cheaper to install, but really only suitable for small greenhouses when low minimum winter temperatures are required. They must be refilled regularly and often, and the heat is not very well distributed so that there are often cold corners in the greenhouse. However, a great many people get satisfactory results this way, and it may be the only way open to many pockets. In fact, a paraffin stove is a very good stand-by in the event of electrical power cuts, which always seem to be arranged for mid-winter and which would have caused many a gardener a broken heart were it not for the timely intervention of paraffin. By the way, if you are considering a paraffin stove, go for one which burns with a blue flame and no fumes, and if possible one which has a receptacle for heating water and thus providing a degree of humidity. Keep the wick clean and not turned up too high.

3. Gas

New gas greenhouse heaters are now being designed and produced, with built-in thermostats and flame-safety valves so that the main burner cannot come on unless the pilot jet is alight. All you have to do is to light the pilot, set the thermostat, and it will turn itself on whenever it is needed.

Until fairly recently the idea of a gas heater amongst his plants – with the possibility of coal gas escaping and causing the loss of his favourite specimens – would be enough to give a keen gardener a heart attack.

Natural gas, however, seems to enrich the greenhouse atmosphere with carbon dioxide (CO_2), which is what many commercial growers do artificially. Published scientific papers support this technique, indicating that the combination of moist warmth and CO_2 can encourage and even increase plant growth tremendously. I have found the thermostatic control to be reliable with little variance, and of course natural gas is a very cheap fuel.

4. Solid fuels

The old-fashioned method of heating greenhouses by means of large cast-iron hot water pipes fired by coal or coke is still very efficient, but the ponderous installations and the fact that they need so much attention have caused them to lose favour with most amateur gardeners. My memories of having to visit the nursery at Merry Hill on cold winters' nights to make sure that the coke-heated boilers were working properly (and to stoke up while I was there) made me then promise myself that it was one form of greenhouse heating I would try to avoid in the future. I have too!

5. Oil-fired air heaters

New models of this type of greenhouse heater have recently been designed for use by the large greenhouse owner or commercial grower. They can also be arranged for tunnel house heating. Complete packaged units are available with aluminium stack pipes, roof plates, cowls, fuel tanks, piping etc. for immediate installation. Lightweight polythene ducting is also available as an optional extra, and the heaters can be fitted with suitable connections if required. They are normally floor standing, fully automatic, thermostatically controlled and easy to maintain, but should only be considered if you have a large glassed area to heat.

Unfortunately nowadays time seems to be such a scarce, important and valuable commodity that much of what we do and have is dominated by consideration of it. I will never understand why there seems to be only half the number of hours in a day as there was when I was a boy! Be that as it may, although our greenhouse is a place for relaxation, we cannot help trying to save time on some jobs so that we can have more time to relax on others. This is why I think, cost apart, thermostatically controlled electric and gas greenhouse heaters will be the most popular for a long time to come – at least until solar heat can be properly harnessed and stored.

5 General greenhouse management

The art of maintaining conditions of growth at their best in a greenhouse calls for careful consideration and judgment of weather conditions and their implications, and applying the resultant knowledge to the general management of your greenhouse. Working in constant close contact with the plants in your greenhouse, you will find yourself gradually getting to know them as living individuals (this is a very pleasant process) and come to learn their moods and their needs. Most of the time we are trying to train the plants to live in artificial conditions, and to be successful we should never forget these basic requirements of nature which must be listed under the heading of Greenhouse Management:

1. Temperature.
2. Humidity.
3. Ventilation.
4. Light (and shade).
5. Hygiene.
6. Protection against pests and diseases.
7. Feeding.

In a greenhouse you are able to control the 'climate' to a great extent and provide the most desirable conditions for the type of plants being grown. You do this by providing a suitable temperature, ventilation, moisture and shade as and when required.

1. Temperature

Some plants can tolerate fairly wide fluctuations of temperature without coming to harm, but the gardener should always be aware of the limits which he can allow for the species being grown. A good maximum/minimum thermometer hung in the greenhouse just above staging level should be used to give the highest and lowest temperatures – usually at 12-hourly intervals – the thermometer being reset after each reading.

In bright daylight growth activity increases, and therefore a higher temperature is needed, but at night plants will manage quite well with temperatures of some 6°C (10°F) or so less than during the day. Another thing you will notice with experience is that older and more mature plants will resist both unduly low or high temperatures better than young ones. Just like humans!

Seeds usually need higher temperatures to germinate than do the consequent seedlings. Although generally preoccupied with keeping temperatures high enough, don't forget that too much heat can also be damaging to some plants.

2. Humidity

Without a heating system a greenhouse is more difficult to manage, particularly in winter. Damp, stuffy conditions must be avoided when temperatures are low, so the roof ventilators should be opened whenever possible, but don't oper the vents if to do so causes a sudden and severe drop in the greenhouse temperature. During this time watering should be done very sparingly and it is better to keep the soil slightly dry rather than wet.

A heating system is of value not only in maintaining the desired temperatures but also in preventing excessively damp conditions from developing, particularly when the outside weather is cold and damp. For instance, in autumn, when the air is often damp at night a little heat coupled with some roof ventilation will help to overcome the dampness.

In hot summer weather the situation is reversed. To prevent temperatures rising too high inside the greenhouse the ventilators should be opened fully and some shade given with blinds (sometimes called roll shades) or a proprietary colour distemper applied to the outside of the greenhouse roof. In addition, water is sprayed on to the floor and stagings so that it will evaporate and create a more humid atmosphere around the plants. Besides allowing plants to lose moisture too rapidly through transpiration, hot and dry conditions in a greenhouse tend to encourage red spider mites – and what a pest they are! Watering should be freely applied really soaking the plants, especially those which have filled their pots with roots. As water is taken in by the roots, passing through the system of the plant until a great proportion of it is lost by transpiration and evaporation from the leaves, it is also a good idea to spray over the foliage of the plants with a fine mist-spray. This hinders the moisture loss, can prevent flagging, and if the pot soil is not bone dry at the time can sometimes be used instead of watering.

Normally the mist-spraying of the foliage is carried out in conjunction with watering on hot, dry days.

Remember that humidity is a factor closely associated with ventilation, and in general the greenhouse conditions to try and avoid are very dry atmospheres and very stuffy ones. My father used to say 'If you feel comfortable in a greenhouse, the plants will too.'

3. Ventilation

Proper usage of ventilators helps to prevent temperatures rising too high in hot weather, helps to control humidity or dryness and, of course, is so important in the health-giving circulation of air and the introduction of fresh air to the greenhouse.

Ventilation goes hand-in-hand with the control of heat and humidity. There are no hard and fast rules, but normally it is sound practice to open ventilators progressively on days of increasing warmth in the mornings, closing down in the afternoons or early evenings ahead of the temperature falls. Top ventilators are opened first, and then the side if necessary – and remember it must be done without causing draughts and as gradually as possible. (Plants hate sudden changes of temperature.)

On windy days, see that ventilators are only opened on the lee side of the greenhouse, and when in doubt remember that over-ventilation is better than too little. This is something you will soon get used to, with experience of watching the reactions of the plants to your actions.

To keep the air buoyant and fresh it must be changed from time to time. Warm air always rises to the top of the greenhouse, and this movement results in replacement by cooler air lower down. This is why I like the introduction of a louvred vent low down in the greenhouse door so that it will be fresh air to be heated before it begins to rise. This is during the colder weather, of course, when the door is closed and the heat is on.

4. Light (and shade)

With air, water and nutrients, light is one of the essentials to plant growth, so basically, all the plants we normally grow in a greenhouse need ample light. Some however, like orchids, ferns, gloxinia etc. not only need less light but thrive on a degree of shade from strong direct sunlight. From about October to April your greenhouse glass should be kept clean, allowing maximum light to penetrate, but in summer the light and heat from the sun will become too intense for a great many other plants. This is the time when some form of shading must be provided to prevent plants from wilting, and it can be done by painting the glass with some form of proprietary green distemper or fixing 'blinds' or roll shades to the roof.

Once the shade distemper is applied it will stay on until you wash and brush it off in September, but if you are able to fit blinds these can be more easily controlled by rolling up or lowering as required. Remember that although seeds will easily germinate and cuttings will root easily in summer in the greenhouse, it would be disaster to put them on to the staging in the full glare of the blazing sun. An hour of direct sunshine intensified through glass is enough to kill almost anything without an adequate root system. Sometimes larger plants like tomatoes can provide sufficient shade for smaller plants to be grown beneath them.

5. Hygiene

This heading was suggested to me when I heard a friend of mine greet his wife Jean rather frivolously on getting home after a successful day at the office!

Thorough cleanliness is most important in a greenhouse, where dust, dirt – even portions of dead and rotting vegetation – can so quickly accumulate if you are not careful, and if this happens, plant diseases and disorders will soon follow. Try to make a habit of keeping the place clean and tidy, clearing away all the results of your pruning, propagating etc. as soon as you have finished. You'll find that the place will not only look better, but will be a healthier home for your plants.

Wash and disinfect the glass regularly, both inside and out, and it helps to spray down the staging and walls with Jeyes Fluid occasionally. Any grime or dirt on the glass can exclude light, so this is an important job. Use paint or preservative on all timber long before it reaches anywhere near the rotting stage—in other words, keep a close watch on your woodwork which, if neglected, could be a home for pests and disease spores.

Pests and diseases can spread very rapidly in the warmth and protection of a greenhouse, but most can be effectively controlled by using insecticidal or fungicidal smokes and sprays.

If you grow tomatoes, chrysanthemums, carnations, cucumbers etc. in the same greenhouse soil year after year, it will almost certainly become infected with eelworm and spores of various root diseases. These must be destroyed, if good healthy growth is to be ensured, by treating the soil with one of many proprietary chemical sterilants such as formaldehyde. The alternative is completely to change the soil every one or two years, or if tomatoes or chrysanthemums are the crops to consider, grow them by the Ring Culture method.

Loam used for seed sowing and potting must be free from all harmful organisms and sterilisation will help to do this. You can either steam heat the soil or treat it with a chemical sterilant. Most sterilants are liquids, which when applied to the soil change to gases so that its effect is extended for some distance beyond the point of application.

Whilst being simple and straightforward, chemical sterilisation is not as thorough as steam heat treatment, which when properly applied, eliminates all pests, diseases and weed seeds. Chemical sterilants, too, are selective in their action. For example, formaldehyde is more effective against disease spores than pests, and cresylic acid kills pests rather better than it does fungi. That's life, I suppose, but quite honestly both these chemicals do a wonderful job with the greenhouse soil, which should be slightly moist, well cultivated and at a temperature between 16°C and 26°C (60°F and 80°F) for the best results.

Unless you have something like an Electric Steam Sterilisation Unit, steam heat sterilisation of soil can be a very difficult and cumbersome job, but with a little ingenuity a simple unit can be made by resting a circular metal plate covered with small nail holes halfway down a heavy metal bucket. Pour in water up to about 2 in. below the plate level, and fill the top half of the bucket with the soil to be sterilised. Now place the bucket on a stove or gas ring and keep the water boiling so that the only way the steam can escape is through the soil. For the best results the soil should be dry and the steam should be allowed to pass through it for at least 15 minutes.

Don't forget, of course, that pests and diseases can be carried into the greenhouse on tools, pots, boxes, trays etc., so wash them in disinfectant as often as you can.

6. Protection against pests and diseases

Much of this subject has been covered under the heading of 'Hygiene', neglect of which can make it easier for pests and diseases to settle down in your greenhouse. Remember the plants are in your care, and if they are attacked through neglect you must be prepared to do everything to save them.

With the advent of the new systemic insecticides and systemic fungicides, the gardener's lot is made so much easier, for once they get into the system of the plant they cannot be washed off and go on working for weeks on end. Watch out for the instructions on the bottle, though, to learn which plants each individual maker suggests avoiding.

As a general protection, it is a time and labour-saving idea to mix your diluted systemic insecticide and systemic fungicide together in the same receptacle, so that the resultant spray will be effective against both pests and diseases. A fine pressure mist spray is ideal for application to plant foliage, and don't always wait until the pests or diseases are clearly apparent; remember prevention is more effective than cure.

Fumigation is a very good weapon, and can be carried out by electrically operated aerosols or by manually-lit 'smokes' that fill the whole house. Get the correct capacity smoke generator for your greenhouse (multiply length by width by average height between eaves and ridge to give cubic footage) and before lighting it see that the house is shut up tight to prevent the escape of any fumes. As soon as you have ignited the 'smoke', get out of your greenhouse and lock the door so that no one else can get in. Those fumes don't only kill plant pests!

I remember Cyril and I explaining all the above in detail on a TV programme, lighting the smoke, and winding up the programme outside the greenhouse completely oblivious of the fact that grey smoke was rising in clouds in the background. We had left a ventilator open!

Plate 15 Camplex '1 bushel' soil steriliser

Watch out for red spider mite, which is a tiny, troublesome pest closely related to the true spiders. The damage they cause usually takes the form of yellow mottling of the leaves of the host plants which are stunted or killed. These tiny red pests spend the winter hibernating (in the adult mite condition) in cracks and crannies in the greenhouse, favoured places being nail holes, bamboo canes and other similar places. So once again you see how important is greenhouse hygiene. Insecticide 'smokes' and systemic insecticides are both effective in the control of red spider, and azobenzene smoke generators destroy their eggs which are usually laid on greenhouse plants during March and April.

Plate 16   Botrytis damage on tomatoes

A fungus disease to avoid in the greenhouse is grey mould or *Botrytis cinerea*. It is microscopic in size but large quantities of spores show up in the mass as a grey velvety layer which gives the fungus its English name. In cold and wet conditions botrytis can cause a great deal of damage on crops like lettuce, tomatoes, grape vines etc., so be particularly careful of over-watering when the forecast suggests that the night will be cold.

7. Feeding

Under natural conditions plants feed themselves by sending out roots to search for necessary moisture and nutrients. Water makes up about 80 per cent of their weight and the assimilation of carbon dioxide from the air provides a high proportion of the rest of the tissue material. Three elements only – carbon, hydrogen and oxygen are concerned in this conversion, but the remaining 1 or 2 per cent of the plant consists of fifty or sixty different chemical elements, all of which are taken up from the soil.

Fortunately, you do not have to include carbon, hydrogen and oxygen in your feeding programme, nor is there need to add all of the fifty or sixty chemical elements or nutrients since at the present moment we only know of about sixteen chemical elements which are essential for healthy growth. Three only of these – nitrogen, phosphorus and potassium – are required in really large amounts, although sometimes it may be necessary to add some of the other trace elements such as magnesium, calcium, boron, iron etc. in small quantities. So plants, like us, have to eat to live, taking in the chemical elements through the tiny root hairs at the tips of the root system. It is these tiny root hairs that we must be careful not to damage when potting or repotting.

Of the sixteen known elements that are essential for healthy growth only three (nitrogen, phosphorus and potassium) are taken out of the soil in comparatively large amounts, and supplies have to be replenished regularly for good results; in other words, the soil must be fertilised. Calcium and magnesium are sometimes lacking and have to be supplied to the soil in the form of lime and Epsom salts. Sulphur, boron, manganese, iron, copper, zinc, molybdenum, chlorine etc. are needed only in very small amounts or traces – hence their name 'trace elements'.

Each of these chemical elements has a particular job to do. For example, nitrogen is the growth element and promotes healthy lush leaf growth, phosphorus (phosphate) promotes healthy root action and potassium (potash) is the element to increase the flower and fruit yield. No one element can replace the other – you cannot have normal plants when nitrogen is in short supply even though you have given the soil plenty of phosphates and potash. In fact, an excess of one element can often cause symptoms of deficiency of another element to become apparent, e.g. apples and tomatoes sometimes show symptoms of magnesium deficiency when given too much potash.

How much fertiliser? What kind? When to apply? are some of the questions we now have to answer in order to get the best results from our fertilisers. As plants can't talk, their only recourse is to make signs which we must learn to recognise. Quite often these signs denoting deficiencies are easy to see but not always easy to identify since several may show the same symptoms.

Plate 17   Sudbury soil test kit

As we have said before, prevention is much better than cure, so try not to wait for the plants' signs of deficiency and keep them fed during their growing season with a balanced liquid fertiliser.

If you feel that the compost you are using in your greenhouse has a deficiency, use one of the many soil test kits there are on the market; they can be most helpful.

Apart from the nutrients already present in the potting compost, no feeding is necessary immediately after potting or repotting, or any time until the roots are well established. (This does not apply to water, which plants need to help their roots settle into the new compost.)

Never feed a plant when the soil is dry, the temperature is low or the plant is dormant and not actually growing. When feeding greenhouse plants it is always preferable to use a proprietary balanced liquid fertiliser mixed with water, remembering that no roots can take in any fertiliser unless it is completely soluble.

A new way of fertilising a plant is by one of the very efficient foliar feeds now available. These are sprayed on to the foliage with a fine mist spray, and the nutrients are taken in through the pores of the leaves as the plant breathes.

Of course you can even use a foliar feed when the roots are on the dry side or waterlogged, as its goodness

The author
(just checking on a *Fuchsia fulgens*)

Top: Black Hamburgh grapes with a healthy 'bloom'

Above: Campsis radicans – a tender but beautiful greenhouse climber

Above: Alton aluminium lean-to greenhouse on S.W.-facing wall

Insert: Corner of a
greenhouse illustrating
use of Humex Roll-
shades

Right: Well-stocked alpine house at the home of the well-known alpine plant expert, Mr Roy Elliott (note the half clay pots standing on the gravel bed)

Below: Alton 'Windsor' Dutch Light cedar greenhouse with staging one side and glass-to-ground the other

comes down from the leaves irrespective of soil conditions.

It is not a bad idea to make your own liquid fertiliser by suspending a sack or bag full of farmyard manure in a barrel of water (rain-water if possible). Add a little soot to the manure, and let it soak for a week or so before using it when the solution is the colour of weak tea. It makes an excellent organic liquid fertiliser, as also is the well-known fertiliser made from seaweed.

It must be stressed, however, that fertilisers alone are not a cure-all for all gardeners' troubles – they merely supplement the soil's store of nutrients. And not only must the plant be well fed, the roots must have a good home to live in, otherwise fertilisers may lose some of their beneficial effect.

Just a final word on photosynthesis, which – in very simple terms – is the means by which the action of the sun on the chlorophyll in the green leaves converts the nutrients coming up from the roots into carbo-hydrates and other foods to give the plant energy. In other words, photosynthesis is the vital means by which green plants obtain life-giving compounds. It is sometimes known as carbon-assimilation, and is the means of producing oxygen and sugar from carbon dioxide and water by utilising the energy of the sun. It takes place in the parts of the plant containing chlorophyll, such as the leaves and green parts of the stem, and is carried on only during daylight hours.

6 Automation in the greenhouse

Although automation usually means electricity, and we have spoken about the use of automatic heating controlled by thermostats, there are still one or two aids to automation which are not dependent upon a continual supply of electric power.

1. Automatic vent control

This is a unit attached to the greenhouse vent whereby the vent is automatically opened or closed according to the rise or fall of the temperature within the greenhouse. Basically the unit consists of a cylinder containing a carefully-measured quantity of a special compound and a machined piston-rod, with well designed glands and seals to ensure perfect functioning – even in our changeable weather. This special compound is so sensitive that it will expand or contract in response to the slightest change in the temperature, so you see it requires no source of power other than that which it contains itself. The whole unit needs no fuel, no supervision and there are no running costs; and once fitted it can be left to adjust your greenhouse vents quietly and efficiently to suit any changes of temperature as they occur. The unit can be fitted to wood or metal-framed greenhouses to operate both roof and side ventilators. Because of its size and simplicity the cost is not exorbitant, and this is a unit I would unhesitatingly recommend to any greenhouse enthusiast.

2. Automatic watering

There are a number of variations on this theme, based not on electric power but on the principle of capillary action and gravity. I like the automatic capillary watering system designed as an alternative to using sand-filled trays. The function of this system depends largely on the specially-constructed fibre mat which will retain up to one gallon of water per square yard. This is laid over polythene sheeting on the greenhouse staging so that the plants (standing on the fibre mat) can take up the required amount of moisture by capillary action.

Of course, soluble nutrients may be added to the water for feeding as desired.

The best way to use this fibre mat is as follows:

(1) Place a shallow container, such as a sand tray, about 2 in. deep, on to the end of the staging and fill with water.

(2) Spread a sheet of polythene over a board raised to the level of the rim of the shallow container and stand (1) and (2) side by side.

(3) Lay the fibre mat on top of the polythene with one end inserted in the water to its full depth. Taper the mat, by cutting with scissors, if necessary, and make sure that the rest of it does not overlap the edges of the board.

(4) Slowly moisten the mat with a few pints of water which it will absorb and retain.

(5) Place the plant pots on to the fibre mat, leaving them to take up the required amount of moisture by capillary action.

This is a very simple method, but quite effective – the water in the container keeping the fibre mat moist and your plants fresh. Do make sure, however, that the level of the mat is just above the water line in the container, and if clay pots are used it is a good idea to stuff small pieces of the mat into the drainage holes to act as wicks.

Another way of maintaining a water supply to the fibre mat – or to a shallow bench tray filled with sand – is by a light-weight plastic tank fitted above staging level. This can be topped-up periodically by hand or plumbed to the mains water supply and kept continuously full by an interior ball-cock. The supply is then piped down to the mat or sand tray on the staging and controlled by a boxed control valve. Of course this controlled supply of water from the tank can also be used to drip-feed individual plants as required.

Electricity can also play its part where watering is concerned by installing a completely automatic watering system which fully controls the amount and frequency of the watering. The control unit of this system contains a solenoid valve which automatically switches the

Plate 19   Nethergreen automatic watering system with
tank and control valve

mains water supply on and off. A detector probe or electronic 'leaf' is inserted into a special compartment in the unit which can be flooded with water through a porcelain block. As soon as the porcelain block absorbs all the water from its own basin and the probe's compartment, an electrical circuit is made and the solenoid valve turns on the water. As soon as the block and the compartment are flooded, the solenoid switches off and the water ceases to flow. The duration of the water application can be controlled by the adjustment of a special screw which regulations the flow of water to the block and probe compartment. The water to the plants is usually delivered through a perforated plastic pipe connected to one end of the control unit.

In simple terms this complicated jargon more or less means that the moisture-sensitive control unit is able to control the supply of water according to the humidity or dryness of the atmosphere in which the plants are standing. By use of special fine mist spray heads attached to the controlled water supply, this system can be most valuable for propagation purposes. As soon as a cutting is severed from a growing plant it normally starts to wilt due to loss of moisture from the leaf by transpiration. This is overcome with even the most difficult subjects by the installation of an automatic mist propagation unit which maintains a constant degree of moisture in the cutting, preventing it from wilting, and rooting generally occurs after a relatively short time. The film of moisture on the leaf of the cutting has a screening effect on the sun's rays, and this affords a lower leaf temperature which ensures that the metabolic rate is not increased to a degree at which food-reserves are quickly depleted. (In other words, keeping the cutting cooler means that it can survive longer without food until its roots have formed.) The ability to form and develop roots on the cutting is not therefore impaired by lack of energy. However, the moisture in mist form is only reapplied as it is lost from the leaf surface through the action of the moisture detector or electronic leaf. If you are in any way interested in the vegetative propagation of difficult subjects, I would not hesitate to recommend the installation of a mist propagation unit.

3. Lighting
The use of electricity for lighting your greenhouse is important, not only to enable you to tend your plants in the long winter evenings, but also to encourage out-of-season growth for certain plants. There is sometimes a deep-seated but understandable reluctance on the part of the housewife to purchase chrysanthemums or other plants which are offered in flower at a time of the year other than their natural flowering period, but it can be a most interesting operation to carry out in your own greenhouse – and of course a commercially profitable one – if you can succeed in producing such a phenomenon from normal young plants.

The growth of some plants and their flowering and fruiting times can be influence by adjusting or varying the number of hours of light and darkness per day. For this all that is required is low intensity light. Plants can be divided into two types–long-day plants and short-day ones. Increasing the length of day by lighting will induce the flowering of long-day types during natural short daylight hours. Short-day plants such as mid-season and early-flowering chrysanthemums can have their flowering times delayed if a day length of over $14\frac{1}{2}$ hours is provided from mid-August to about mid-October.

It is possible to promote continued growth through artificial light in winter so that new varieties of, say, rhododendrons and azaleas can grow up much more quickly and the results of breeding seen at an earlier date than normal. The production of bloom out of season is quite simple, but some plants are not as sensitive to artificial light as others. Fuchsias, begonias etc. seem to be very responsive.

Long-day plants which require a good length of light time in the day – such as strawberries – are dealt with in this manner in Holland on a commercial scale.

Light is life to a plant. In low winter light, leaves fall from trees, but it is interesting to note that a tree near a street light will retain its leaves longer on the side facing the street light than on the opposite side. There are available specially designed horticultural lamps of various wattages. For the treatment of chrysanthemums, 100-watt lamps may be suspended about 6 ft above the plants and spaced 5 ft to 6 ft apart. More intense lighting of 400 watts is suitable for raising seedlings such as tomatoes early in the season. (Such mercury lamps have an average life of 4000 hours.) For amateur needs 100-watt lamps or multiples of these are quite satisfactory.

Artificial light is ideal for the cultivation of saint-paulias (African violets) and specially designed growing cabinets can be purchased for this purpose. A special strip light fixed in the roof of an electric propagator will encourage more rapid and vigorous growth of seedlings, especially during the duller early spring months. Do remember, however, that only specially

Fig. 2 Construction of screened soil/air warming cable

manufactured apparatus and fittings should be used, and unless you are one yourself, a competent electrician should always be called in to carry out the installation.

4. Soil warming

In Chapter 4 we discussed various ways of controlled or automated greenhouse heating, but soil warming by screened electric cables is a technique which can be used in an unheated greenhouse or even a cold frame. Soil warming greatly increases the scope and interest for the horticulturist, and enables him not only to produce early crops but also to raise seedlings and plants, and to strike cuttings which require some artificial bottom heat. The chance of success in the rooting of cuttings of most evergreens, and especially conifers, is greatly increased by the employment of soil-warming cables, which can, of course, also be used in conjunction with a mist propagating unit. Even in a cold house, a soil-warmed propagating bench will give surprising results, but in a heated greenhouse a bench with soil warming will help to maintain a good air temperature more easily.

As a rough guide, the following lengths and wattage of soil-warming cables are suggested to cover the staging areas listed:

Area 6 to 12 sq. ft. .. Cable 20 ft. at 75 watts
  „ 15 to 24   „   ..   „   40 ft. at 150   „
  „ 30 to 48   „   ..   „   80 ft. at 300   „
  „ 60 to 96   „   ..   „ 160 ft. at 650   „

The above cables can be made to cover larger areas than specified, but the running times would be increased and soil heating may not be so uniform. However, by following the suggested dosages with each cable, it should be possible to obtain a rise in soil temperature of up to nearly 7°C (12°F). To control the soil heat automatically a rod type adjustable soil thermostat may be installed; this usually has an external knob for setting the temperature required.

When installing soil-warming cables, these should be laid 4 in. to 6 in. beneath the surface of the soil and spaced evenly over the area to be warmed. Take care to avoid sharp bends which might damage the cable, and see that the spacing between adjacent runs is not less than 4 in. and not more than 8 in. The cable must never be allowed to cross over itself nor cross any other adjacent cables. If this happens the cable or cables may break down at the point of contact due to overheating, and for the same reason the cable must not be switched on when coiled. To ensure that the warmth dissipated from the cable is evenly distributed throughout the hotbed, the soil should be kept damp at all times.

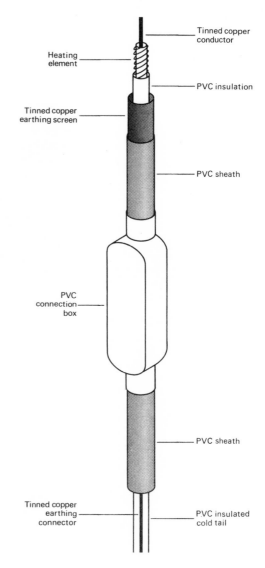

Tinned copper conductor

Heating element

PVC insulation

Tinned copper earthing screen

PVC sheath

PVC connection box

PVC sheath

Tinned copper earthing connector

PVC insulated cold tail

Plate 20   Camplex greenhouse control panel

5. Control panel

If you really go in for the electrical side of automation in the greenhouse, a logical ultimate can be the installation of a control panel to simplify the control of your other installations. Fused circuits, 13 amp. and 5 amp., are incorporated in the panel, and each one is provided with a separate switch and neon indicator lamp. A 60 amp. heavy duty mains switch is fitted, together with weatherproof nylon cable glands, and the whole greenhouse control panel is housed in an insulated PVC case.

One final word of advice on this subject – please remember that water is a very good conductor of electricity, and as any insufficiently-insulated wire or joint is a potential danger, always see that electrical installations are carried out by a competent electrician. You have been warned!

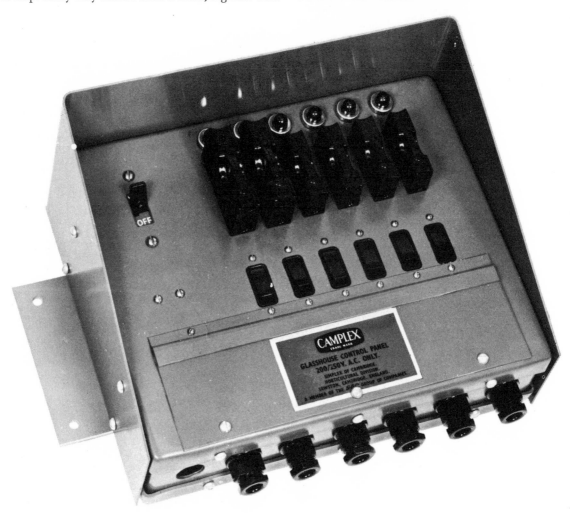

Fig. 3   A typical soil-warmed propagating bench

7 Propagation

Plant propagation plays a very important part in the life of the genuine gardener or keen horticulturist. In many cases it is merely imitating or even furthering the methods used by nature herself. Seeds of plants scattered by the almost violent bursting open of some seed pods, distributed by the wind (here one thinks of the wonderful airborne seeds of such things as dandelion, sycamore etc.) or wiped from the beaks of birds after they have eaten the fleshy seed covering of the berries or fruit – these fall to the ground where those which survive germinate and grow successfully. The reason for this effective germination which often takes place under quite inhospitable conditions is that most seeds like to be sown as soon as possible after they reach ripeness and are ready to part company with the parent plant. This particularly applies to many alpine plants, but there are exceptions – one which springs to mind is the gentian, the seeds of which like to experience a few degrees of frost before they are ready to germinate. Then there are the seeds contained in the berries of holly, cotoneaster etc. which seem to germinate better if first of all stratified, i.e. buried in a clay pot filled with sand and left outside to experience a winter of weather. When you think of it, all these things are just man's poor way of imitating the wonders of nature, without whom no growth or even life would exist. One old gardener once told me 'Never fight nature, always go along with her – she'll win in the end!' We who work alongside nature and try never to oppose her recognise that as a simple yet profound statement of fact.

But of course, the majority of the easier-to-germinate annuals and perennials are packed when freshly harvested in hermetically-sealed packets, distributed through shops and garden centres, and grown very successfully the following season.

Propagation can be effected by seed, cuttings, layers, division, grafting, budding etc., in many cases without any artificial heat whatever. We shall only dwell here, though, on the techniques of propagation where the natural process is helped by the protection of the greenhouse, artificial heat and the prevention of loss of moisture by such methods as the mist propagation unit.

Firstly let's talk about a greenhouse propagating bed set on the staging. This should be about 6 in. deep and the base covered by 1½ in. of damp sand. Soil-warming cables (as discussed in Chapter 6) should then be laid on top of this layer of sand, and finally a further 3 in. thick layer of damp sand should be placed over the cable. An 18 in. rod type thermostat could then be fixed to the side of the bed, with the rod protruding into the upper layer of damp sand. Although this would automatically control the temperature of the sand, it is not an absolute necessity. Seed boxes should stand in the sand and be packed closely together. When pots or seed pans are used they should be plunged ½ in. into the sand. Keep the sand damp at all times, but on no account must the soil-warming cables be laid so as to be in direct contact with any insulating materials such as peat, moss, ashes, vermiculite, fibre, etc. or they may overheat and break down. On top of the bed of sand, however, you may put a mixture of peat and sand for the rooting of cuttings. (Bottom heat is a great help in this operation.) Then above the propagating bed you may install a mist propagation unit with a humidity-controlling electronic leaf, and with all these aforementioned aids to propagation, plus a little experience, even the most difficult of subjects will succumb to your charm!

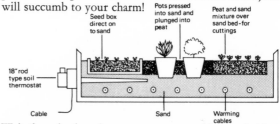

Wait though, there is one even more sophisticated aid to propagation and that is an all-electric PVC dome-covered seed propagator and plant irradiator. In spite of its name

Plate 21   Camplex seed propagator with dome and
plant irradiator

it is just as effective for rooting cuttings. Its size can vary between about 3 ft × 2 ft and 4 ft × 2½ ft, and it consists of a 10 in. deep high density polythene base covered by a removable clear PVC dome. The temperature is maintained automatically by a sensitive 18 in. rod-type thermostat which can be set to operate between 10°C and 21°C (50°F and 70°F). The heating is by means of a 75-watt voltage sheathed soil-warming cable incorporating an earthing screen for safety. On top of this a fluorescent plant irradiator provides supplementary lighting for growing during the winter, so what more could you ask? Your plants will be literally queueing up to be propagated in this, and remember that it can be almost as effective in a cold greenhouse as in a heated one so long as you are careful to keep the young plants warm when you take them out.

1. Seeds

Seeds can be sown in shallow boxes (plastic or wooden, but if the latter first wash them in a mild disinfectant), pots or clay seed pans. Clay pans are good because they absorb moisture and release it back into the soil as it dries out, and for that reason always soak new clay receptacles in water for two or three hours before being used. First of all cover all drainage holes or cracks with 'pot crocks', and fill up with John Innes seed compost or a proprietary soilless seed compost. (If you have neither of these handy, a good substitute is a mixture of one

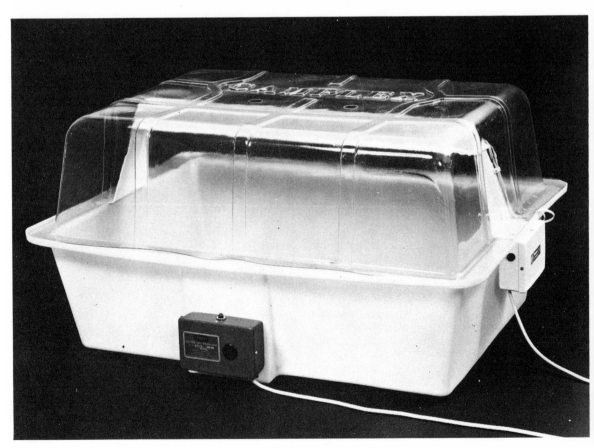

Fig. 4   The correct way to sow seeds thinly in a box

Top
Fig. 5   Compressing compost in a seed tray with a wooden pressing board

Bottom
Fig. 6   Pricking out seedlings

part each – by bulk, not weight – of sifted loam, sharp sand and granulated peat.) Firm the compost with your fingers and level off the top with a strip of wood. A wooden pressing board completes the task of consolidating the compost, which is then watered thoroughly using a fine rose on the can, and set aside to drain. Sow the seeds thinly over the moist surface,

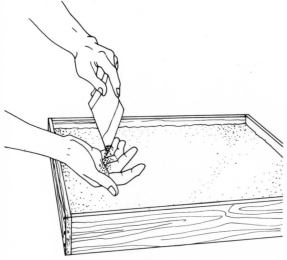

and cover them by sieving a ¼ in. layer of the compost over them. Some seed such as petunia, cyclamen etc., need hardly any covering at all. To germinate, seeds normally need warmth, moisture and darkness, so the container in which we have sown our seed is now covered with a sheet of glass over which a sheet of newspaper (or brown paper) is laid. The glass prevents too much loss of moisture by evaporation and lessens the need for further watering. Even so, the glass should be turned over and wiped dry each day, and if further watering is needed it should be done from the bottom. The paper, of course, provides the dark conditions, and you supply the warmth.

Remove the paper as soon as there is any sign of germination, and raise the glass slightly with short pegs. When the true leaves appear lift the seedlings (by a leaf, not the stem) by easing them out with a pencil or point of a wooden label and carefully transplant them to

another box or pan at wider spacing. This is called 'pricking out'. The next stage is to plant them out if they are hardy annuals or perennials, or transplant them to small pots containing a John Innes potting compost, either No. 1 or No. 2.

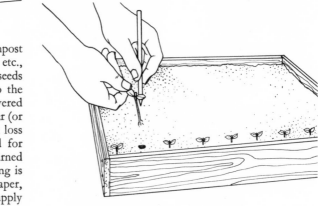

Providing you have a heated greenhouse or seed propagator, you can start sowing seeds of coleus, streptocarpus, begonias etc. in January and February,

49

D

Plate **22** Impatiens (Busy Lizzie)

carrying on with a succession of sowings throughout the year – through May and June with exacum, impatiens, etc., *Cyclamen persicum* in the autumn, and so on. If you look on the underside of the leaves of some indoor ferns in summer you may find them covered with small brown spots. These are seed spores and it is best to remove the leaves bearing them to be stood on a clean white sheet of paper on the greenhouse staging. After a while the leaves may be lightly shaken, leaving the spores on the paper. These may be sown carefully on a peat/sand mixture, hardly covered at all (other than for darkness) and treated as tender seeds.

Fig. 7 A typical nodal cutting

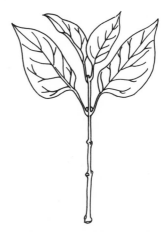

If your greenhouse is heated but you have no electric seed propagator, there are some excellent yet inexpensive clear Perspex covers available to fit ordinary pots or seed trays. Some of these are fitted with controllable air vents, but all have a beneficial effect on seed germination. Do not be surprised if plants grown from seed show a slight variance from the parent plant – this can be the result of cross-pollination by bees and other insects and can sometimes turn out to be an improvement.

2. Cuttings

A cutting is some part of a plant, usually a side shoot from a main stem, which, when gently but firmly inserted in a rooting medium such as a mixture of equal parts (by bulk) of sharp sand and granulated peat, develops into a new plant identical to its parent. This is called vegetative propagation, which can also include *root cuttings* (phlox, anchusa, *Anemone japonica* etc.) and *leaf cuttings* (*Begonia rex*, saintpaulia etc.) *Stem cuttings* may be of either 'hard' wood, 'semi-ripe' wood or 'soft' wood, often depending on species and time of year. These may be further broken down into types of stem cuttings – 'nodal', 'inter-nodal' and 'heel'. A nodal cutting is one which is cut with a clean sharp knife or razor blade immediately below a node or leaf joint. Cleanly cut off (not break) the lower leaves, leaving one or two pairs at the top, and insert about one-third of its depth into moist sandy soil, any proprietary cutting compost, a sand/peat mix as mentioned above or in a propagating bed or seed propagator. Until rooted, they should be shaded from direct sunlight and (unless you have a mist propagating unit installed) be lightly sprayed over with tepid water each morning, besides keeping the rooting medium damp. Any cuttings that show signs of damping off should be removed. This procedure also applies to a *heel* cutting, which is a short side stem taken by plucking it off, at a point where it joins the main stem, with a sharp downward pull, taking a fragment of the main stem with it, the soft torn skin of which is trimmed off with a sharp knife. Stem cuttings, whether heel or nodal, should be of firm short-jointed shoots of the current season's growth which have not flowered. The length of the cutting often depends on the kind of plant – cuttings of chrysanthemums, dahlias, pelargoniums (geraniums) would be anything from 2½ in. to 4 in. long.

Geraniums (which are, of course, botanically pelargoniums) can be taken at almost any time of the year in a heated greenhouse or propagator, but I find that September-rooted cuttings are best. When you have taken your geranium cuttings, leave them on a piece of clean paper on the staging for an hour or so before inserting them. This reduces their chances of 'damping off', a condition denoted by the stem of the cutting turning black. In the spring young shoots may be taken from the base of such plants as dahlias and chrysanthemums which have been forced into early growth in a heated greenhouse. These are soft stem cuttings and after they have been prepared by trimming them cleanly below a node or the harder base of the stem at soil level and removing the lower leaves, they should be inserted in a moist rooting medium at a temperature of about 13°C (55°F).

Clematis are plants which are usually propagated by *inter-nodal* cuttings, i.e. cuttings taken from half-way between two nodes or leaf-joints, and if good semi-ripe growth is used you will be surprised how easily they will root.

Indoor house plants such as dieffenbachia, dracaena etc. may be propagated by cutting the main stem into short lengths or sections, so long as each section bears a growing bud or eye. These are pushed vertically into small pots of a peat/sand compost (one to a pot) so that the top of the stem protrudes a little above the compost, and if this is kept warm and moist, rooting will take place in a matter of weeks.

To set all the above-mentioned cuttings, make a small hole in the rooting medium with a pencil or pointed stick, insert the cutting about a third of its length and press firmly all around it, making sure that the base of the cutting is in firm intimate contact with the mixture. Cuttings, unlike seeds, seem to welcome company and seem to do better when planted as close together as possible. Dip their tips into a rooting hormone powder before inserting them to encourage a good start and reduce the risk of failure, but even this is not absolutely necessary with such easy subjects as hydrangeas, carnations etc. However, until you get more confidence with experience, it's better to be on the safe side.

Subsequent treatment of the cuttings is to keep them in a close humid atmosphere. The dome-covered propagator is ideal, as is the Perspex-covered pan or seed tray, but if you have neither of these most cuttings are quite happy in a pot covered by an upturned polythene bag which is supported above the cuttings by two crossed bent wires and held to the side of the pot by an elastic band. (Here I must mention the fact – and it is a fact – that most cuttings root more successfully if inserted around the edge of the pot than if just distributed over the area of the top of the pot.) Providing this close atmosphere is supplied, there are a number of plant cuttings which require no heat if taken in summer. These include hydrangeas, fuchsias, dianthus etc. etc.

Propagation by *leaf cuttings* is successful with numerous plants, including gloxinias, saintpaulias, *Begonia rex*, streptocarpus etc. With saintpaulias, the leaf is removed with about ¾ in. stem which is inserted in a moist peat/sand compost and kept warm and humid, though care must be taken to see that the actual leaves are not wetted or they rot.

With the others mentioned, remove a healthy well-developed leaf from the parent plant, make a few light incisions with a sharp knife across the veins on the underside and then lay the leaf on the surface of a moist ·compost consisting of a mixture of equal parts (by bulk) of sharp sand and granulated peat. If your wife isn't looking, peg the leaf down with hairpins – otherwise use bent wires. It is desirable that all parts of the leaf should be in contact with the compost. Leaf cuttings should be shaded from direct sunlight and be kept in a reasonably warm and moist atmosphere. Obviously, with so much leaf area exposed, loss by

transpiration could be excessive, so care must be taken to restrict this. However, roots often form quite quickly by this method, but be extra careful when potting on as these roots are invariably most tender.

Christmas cactus cuttings may be rooted in May or June. Use a sandy compost. Each cutting should consist of a branching 'frond' of four or five leaf pads. After making a clean cut, insert the lower half of the bottom leaf into the compost, and rooting should soon take place.

The sansevieria or, as it is sometimes unkindly called, 'Mother-in-Law's-Tongue', may be propagated by cutting the long fleshy leaves into short lengths of about 3 in. and inserting them into a moist sandy compost around the edge of a pot.

As a result of our TV programme, I often get letters from friends (there are no such things as strangers, they're only friends you haven't met) saying that their rubber plant has grown so high that it is touching the ceiling. I usually write and suggest that they have two alternatives, either saw a hole in the ceiling or cut the plant down to about 18 in. from soil level, keeping it watered and fed to induce new side shoots and make what I think would be a bushier and better plant. You are wondering, I expect, what this has to do with propagation – but think for a moment of that 6 ft or more of stem and leaves of *Ficus elastica* lying on the living room carpet, to all intents its life and purpose snuffed out with one snick of the secateurs. This need not be so, because the ficus is propagated by *leaf-bud cuttings* which means that every healthy leaf attached to that long stem lying there can be transformed into a new plant.

With a very sharp knife or secateurs cut the main stem about ½ in. below and again ½ in. above each leaf joint or node, making a leaf-bud cutting consisting of a leaf and a 1 in. hammer-head of stem. Every leaf will then make a separate cutting, each of which is potted singly into 3 in. pots of moistened rooting medium. Bury the main stem-piece with just the leaf above soil level, put in a propagator or cover with a polythene bag, and if kept warm and moist rooting will soon take place. By the way, let the milky latex fluid dry off from the cuts in the stem and then dip in a rooting hormone powder before you insert the cutting.

Camellias are also increased by *leaf-bud cuttings* which are taken from the current year's growth, complete with

Plate 23   Saintpaulia (African Violet)

a leaf and plump dormant bud with a small piece of stem wood attached. These are inserted in sharp, moist sand in March or April in gentle heat, but to minimise the chance of failure a mist propagation unit is a great help in the case of camellias.

Another way of propagating varieties of ficus, dracaena, dieffenbachia, magnolia etc. is by *air layering*. An upward slanting cut is made in the main stem opposite a node, and rooting hormone powder is dusted into the the cut with a small paint brush. Damp sphagnum moss

Plate 24 *Begonia rex*

is then packed into and around the cut, polythene is wrapped firmly around the moss, and tied above and below with sticky tape to keep the whole process air and water-tight. Healthy young pencil-thick shoots of ripe wood of the previous year's growth – not old, hard wood – should be chosen for air layering, and April or May seem to be the best months for it to be carried out. If the shoot which you have air layered is not very strong, a short, thin piece of cane attached to the shoot above and below would provide adequate support. When the roots form and can be seen in the moss, the layer is severed from the parent plant, but do be careful when removing the polythene and potting up as the new roots will be very tender and fragile. Ground and air layering are usually reliable methods of propagation as while the new roots are forming the layer or cutting is still receiving sustenance from the parent plant – a sort of umbilical principle!

8 House plants to grow ~ and how

At the very start of this book we mentioned the close liaison between family, home and greenhouse – keeping the home looking nice and the family happy just by the constant supply of fresh house plants from the greenhouse without eating too much into the family budget. This is not a pipe dream, it can be a reality – all you need is a little incentive, some seeds, tubers, bulbs or even cuttings from friends and you are away on the merry-go-round, nursing back to health plants which have deteriorated whilst being in the house, and replacing them with fresh healthy plants from the greenhouse.

Like all of us, house plants all have their likes and dislikes – and one of their pet aversions is draughts. You see, they do not like suffering from extremes of temperature and that is just what draughts cause. Often a lower temperature is more acceptable to a house plant, provided it is constant, than a higher which varies.

Remember, too, that the natural habitat of many house plants is the tropical and sub-tropical jungles of the world, where the air is warm and humid, so that it is quite understandable if these same plants begin to wilt in the dry centrally-heated rooms of our modern houses. One way of introducing a degree of humidity around an individual plant is as follows:

Stand the pot on a saucer filled with ¼ in. washed gravel, but only half-filled with water. The air will then be allowed to circulate through the dry top half of the gravel and the pot drainage holes into the compost, and the water in the lower half of the gravel in the saucer will evaporate in the warmth of the room and create a humid atmosphere around the plant itself. Another method is to spray the foliage daily with a fine mist spray containing water at room temperature.

Of course, never forget to feed your house plants with a liquid fertiliser, especially during the time when they are producing new growth or flowers. Again like us, they need more food when they expend more energy, which they do when producing flowers etc. Try to

remember, too, that most plants like to rest for two to three months every year, when feeding should be discontinued and watering reduced to a point where the plants are just being kept alive and in hibernation. Like us having a holiday, it's their time to relax and recharge their batteries.

Watering is so important because no roots can take in any fertiliser unless it is completely soluble, but at the same time if the compost in the pot becomes so saturated with water that all air is excluded then the roots cannot breathe and the plant dies from strangulation. Obviously, a delicate balance must be achieved by virtually only giving the plant a drink when it is thirsty. Try this with your house plants:

'Feel the soil in the top of the pot with your finger every morning (or evening, but at about the same time every day) and unless it is bone dry, don't water. If it *is* bone dry fill the pot up to the rim with rain-water at greenhouse/room temperature and let it drain through the compost.'

In this way, you never leave your plants too dry for more than 24 hours. It is more harmful than good for a plant to give it a few drops of water every day – the small amount of moisture will only sink about ½ in. into the compost and cause the water-starved roots to turn and start growing towards the surface seeking sustenance. If they do reach the surface they are scorched and damaged by the hot, dry atmosphere. So when you do water, really fill the pot sufficiently for it to soak right through the compost.

Remember, by the way, that coal gas fumes are normally death to most house plants, but not natural gas.

Obviously it would be impossible in one chapter to describe or even include, all the plants which can be grown in a greenhouse, so I will try to select those which have earned their popularity through being not only attractive and decorative but also fairly easy to grow. Let's take them in alphabetical order:

Plate 25   Achimenes

Achimenes

Gay, easy and long-lasting flowers of blue, purple or pink produced on plants about 18 in. high which are grown from tubers planted in early spring. According to planting time, the flowers are produced any time between July and September, and the stems need light support unless planted in a hanging basket. Belongs to the gloxinia family, and sometimes called the Hot Water Plant because in the early stages of growth they prefer to be watered with warm water. Achimenes need shade from the bright sunshine during the summer months and a fairly moist atmosphere. In winter when the flowers have faded and the leaves begin to wither, watering must be discontinued gradually and finally, when the leaves have all fallen, the tops are cut off and the soil left dry. Throughout the winter months the tuberous roots are left in their pots or baskets in a minimum temperature of 10°C (50°F), to be taken out and repotted in February or March.

Plate 26 Adiantum

Adiantum cuneatum (Maidenhair fern)
This delightful fern requires a semi-shaded warm greenhouse with a moist atmosphere where the light is diffused, but not too dull. It has small, delicate green leaves carried on wiry black stems, and in the house likes to be kept reasonably cool, moist and free from draughts. A minimum temperature of 10°C to 13°C (50°F to 55°F) is quite suitable. Do not syringe, as the moisture collects between the young fronds and causes them to damp off. Maidenhair ferns can be grown in a window which gets little or no direct sunlight, but usually they deteriorate after a few weeks unless they are taken back to the warm moist greenhouse for a spell. An ideal compost in which to grow them could consist of equal parts of fibrous peat, leafmould and rotted turf loam, with a free scattering of silver sand and a few small pieces of charcoal.

Anthurium
Hothouse plants, chiefly from tropical America, which belong to the arum family and are grown for the sake of their brilliantly-coloured flower spathes. These bright red spathes form a background or shield to the real spiky flower which often looks like a pig's tail. Anthuriums need a minimum greenhouse temperature of 15°C (60°F)

Plate 27   Anthurium

Plate 28   Aphelandra

with a fairly humid atmosphere. Pot on early in the year into well-crocked 6 in. to 7 in. pots filled with a peat-based compost. If you want to mix your own, a suitable compost would consist of 3 parts peat, 1 part leafmould, 1 part sphagnum moss with a scattering of crushed charcoal and coarse sand. Water anthuriums freely in spring and summer and damp down frequently to maintain a moist atmosphere. Shade from direct sunshine. Water and damp down less in autumn and winter, but keep up temperature. Divide and repot in February/March, keeping the crown of the plant well above the compost.

Aphelandra (Zebra plant)

A South American plant with large, shiny olive-green leaves covered with a fantastic pattern of clear creamy-white veins. Distinctive though this feature is, this isn't the plant's only attraction for during the summer months it also bears striking spires of yellow flowers emerging from orange bracts. Plants raised from seeds or cuttings may be planted in well-crocked pots of John Innes Potting Compost No. 2 or any peat-based no-soil compost. In summer keep the greenhouse moist and warm but be careful not to overwater the compost,

Araucaria excelsa

Also known as The Norfolk Island Pine, its good temper and reliability makes it a favourite room and greenhouse plant. A miniature indoor pine tree with regular tiers of soft-leaved branches which will grow from 3 ft to 5 ft, but would not survive out of doors in this country. Will grow in sun or shade, and needs plenty of water in spring but less in winter. In saying what a great little house plant this is, it may be interesting to know that in its natural state this tree would grow as tall as our own Scots pine.

Azalea indica (The Indian Azalea)

Popular evergreen flowering shrubs usually bearing an abundance of mauve, white, pink or red flowers. Buy as flowering plant in winter, and when the flowers begin to fade, carefully pinch them off to prevent them from going to seed. Keep feeding and watering (with rain-water, as azaleas do not relish the lime in tap-water) to induce new growth which, during the summer, should mature and form new buds for the next winter's flowering. To this end, stand the plant outside in a sheltered partially-shaded place from May to September. Keep it well watered and syringe the foliage daily, feeding once a fortnight with a liquid fertiliser. Return it to the greenhouse at the end of September, in a minimum temperature of 10°C (50°F). Repot after flowering, using 3 parts peat, 1 part lime-free loam and 1 part coarse sand.

Begonia

This covers a wide range of both flowering and foliage plants, all highly decorative, long lasting and comparatively easy. *Begonia rex* is grown for its beautifully coloured leaves and propagated as explained in the previous chapter. It likes to be grown in John Innes Potting Compost No. 2 in a warm greenhouse, fed fortnightly in summer when it should also be watered freely, but only watered sparingly in winter.

Then there are the winter-flowering begonias (one popular variety is 'Gloire de Lorraine') and these need a minimum temperature of 15°C (60°F). The double-

Plate 30b   Begonias in greenhouse

Plate 31 *Azalea indica*

flowered varieties of the tuberous-rooted begonia make excellent pot plants and the small-flowered 'pendula' varieties are equally attractive in hanging baskets. Both can be grown from seed or tubers, and the colours range from white and yellow to orange, and from pink through to crimson. Start tubers in February/March by half burying them in trays of moist peat in a temperature of 15 °C (60°F). When small leaves have formed, pot them on in John Innes Potting Compost No. 2. They can be used as individual pot plants or planted out later as summer bedding.

Plate 32   *Beloperone guttata* (Shrimp plant)

Beloperone guttata (The Shrimp plant)
The combination of the lobster-pink flowers and brown-ish-rose bracts gives a shrimp-like effect from which the plant is given its local name. It can be propagated from cuttings set in a sandy mix in spring in a temperature of 15°C (60°F). A seed propagator or propagating frame would be ideal. Give full light for good colour and keep just moist in a fairly warm greenhouse.

Brunfelsia
Low-growing evergreen flowering shrub from tropical America which should be grown in a minimum green-house temperature of 10°C (50°F). Belongs to the potato family, *solanaceae*, grows about 2 ft high, has woody stems and thick, dark green oval leaves, and bears rich purple flowers in terminal clusters. Grown in large pots containing John Innes Potting Compost No. 2 or a peat-based compost, they flower almost continuously if kept shaded in a humid atmosphere during the summer. Water freely in spring and summer, as well as syringing the foliage, but less frequently during the winter. Prune lightly each spring, and increase by cuttings of firm young shoots taken in June or July.

Plate 33   Brunfelsia

Plate 34 Calceolaria

Calceolarias

The greenhouse calceolarias all have large pouched flowers in a variety of colours including red, scarlet, crimson, yellow and orange. They should be grown as biennials to be renewed from seed annually, and belong to the same botanical family as the snapdragon. Sow seed in May or June and leave seedlings, pricked out, shaded from direct sunlight but watered freely and given ample ventilation, in a cold frame until mid-September. Pot them on into 4 in. or 5 in. pots in John Innes Potting Compost No. 2 and through the winter keep them in the greenhouse in a minimum temperature of about 7°C (45°F). In winter go gently with the watering, but gradually increase it in the spring.

Plate 35   Cineraria

Chlorophytum comosum 'Variegatum' (Spider plant)
A greenhouse plant from Africa with long grass-like leaves, striped green and white, arching in a tuft from the tuberous roots. The small white flowers are produced on the end of slender stalks, which also seem to bear self-rooting baby plants. These may be layered into a 3 in. pot of John Innes Potting Compost No. 2 to produce new plants. An interesting and rewarding plant, growing under almost all conditions, and is quite happy in a minimum winter temperature of 7°C (45°F). They make good hanging-basket plants and belong to the lily family.

Cinerarias
Although these are actually herbaceous perennials, they are almost invariably grown from seed as biennials, being discarded after flowering. The daisy-like flowers in a range of rich colours, are produced in fine massed heads from November to May according to the time of sowing. Sow seed in April, May or June in a temperature of about 13°C (55°F), prick out and grow through summer in an unheated greenhouse, the plants being shaded from direct sunlight. From late September onwards keep plants (not then shaded) in a minimum greenhouse temperature of 8°C (47°F). Give them plenty of light and ventilation, as in a stuffy warm, damp atmosphere cinerarias are liable to rot off at soil level. For some reason they seem to be a magnet to white and greenfly, so spray with a systemic insecticide at the first sign of pests.

Plate 36 *Citrus mitis*

Citrus mitis (The Calamondin Orange)
Citrus is the botanical name for all the oranges, lemons, and grapefruits, any of which may be grown as greenhouse plants. The best, however, as it is so neat in habit and usually the most prolific, is *Citrus mitis*, The Calamondin Orange. Like other kinds it has shiny evergreen leaves and white, sweetly-scented flowers, followed by small edible fruits like tangerines. All varieties of citrus can be grown in a well-ventilated greenhouse having a minimum winter temperature of 10°C (50°F), and may be placed outdoors in a sunny, sheltered position from June to September. Water freely in spring and summer, moderately in autumn and sparingly in winter. Sunshine is essential to ripen the fruits and citrus only need light pruning. Increase by summer cuttings of firm young growths or sow ripened pips as seeds. The Calamondin

Orange is a really fascinating plant to grow, often bearing fruit and fragrant flowers at the same time.

Coleus
Beautiful foliage plants with multi-coloured nettle-like leaves in a host of shapes and patterns. Keep warm and well watered, and pinch off all the little insignificant flowers as they appear or the leaves will begin to lose the brilliance of their colours. Sow seed in March or April in a proprietary seed compost in a temperature of about 18°C (65°F), and prick out into John Innes Seed Compost No. 2. If you want to increase a favourite hybrid, cuttings of young side shoots root readily in late summer. Coleus are natives of Indonesia and Africa and belong to the nettle family.

Plate 37   Coleus (mixed)

Cyclamen persicum

There is no denying the fact that this is one of the most popular of Christmas-flowering plants. Actually the lovely butterfly-like flowers are produced from autumn to spring, and an added attraction is the carpet of heart-shaped leaves marbled with silver from which

the flowers arise. Sow seed in August in John Innes seed compost or peat-based seed compost in an unheated greenhouse. Germination may be irregular so carefully lift out the seedlings as they reach the two-leaf stage and prick them out into a similar compost. Grow them through the winter in a greenhouse with a

69

Plate 38   *Cyclamen persicum*

minimum temperature of 7°C (45°F), watering rather sparingly, and pot what are now small corms singly into 3 in. pots in March or April. At this stage, maintain a minimum temperature of 10°C (50°F) and water more freely. In June pot on into 5 in. pots of John Innes Potting Compost No. 2 or peat-based compost and keep the greenhouse well ventilated. From September maintain a minimum temperature of 13°C (55°F) and your flowers should be produced by Christmas.

Euphorbia pulcherrima

Better known as poinsettia, this is another beautiful plant associated with Christmas, but perhaps a little more difficult to grow successfully than the cyclamen. The beauty of this plant lies in the brilliant scarlet bracts which surround the insignificant yellowish flowers. Spring-taken cuttings may be rooted in a seed propagator, and potted singly into 4 in. pots of John Innes Potting Compost No. 2. Water freely through the summer, and include a few drops of a liquid fertiliser about every ten days. Water moderately in autumn and winter, maintaining a minimum temperature of 13°C (55°F). Poinsettias do not like too pronounced a change in atmosphere, so if you bring them into the house at Christmas don't leave them for more than a few weeks before returning them to the greenhouse.

Plate 39   *Poinsettia mikkelrochford*

Plate 40   Freesias (mixed)   Plate 41   *Fuchsia fulgens*

Freesias

Grown from small bulbs, freesias enhance the cool greenhouse with their gracefulness and fragrance.

Plant in August or September six or seven corms 1½ in. deep in 5 in. pots of John Innes Potting Compost No. 2, with plenty of crocks at the bottom for good drainage. After planting, stand in a cold frame or outdoors in a sheltered position, on a bed of ashes or gravel; but the pots should not be covered as is usually done with other bulbs. Water sparingly until top growth develops.

Before the frosts come, the pots should be taken into the cool greenhouse, stood close to the glass and a few twigs inserted around the pots to support the young foliage. Remove any extra growth appearing in the pots to direct the energy of the plant to the main flowering stems. When the flower spikes are seen, apply weak liquid manure at ten-day intervals. Maintain a temperature of around 10°C (50°F) as too much heat in the early stages can cause blindness. Flowering normally begins in February and carries on through the spring.

Fuchsias

Greenhouse fuchsias are very accommodating plants as, apart from flowering almost continuously from May to October, they can be grown as bushes, standards or in hanging baskets. Cuttings of firm young shoots will root easily in a propagator at almost any time from spring to autumn. As soon as they have a sufficient root system pot the rooted cuttings singly into 3 in. pots of John Innes Potting Compost No. 1, and later pot on in 5 in. pots of John Innes Potting Compost No. 2. Water freely when growing and flowering are in full swing in spring and summer, and very sparingly in winter if the greenhouse is inadequately heated – otherwise normal winter watering if a minimum temperature of 10°C (50°F) can be maintained. No artificial heat is, of course, necessary from May to October. Shade from strong direct sunlight and ventilate freely. Most varieties may be planted outside from May to September and some (such as *F. riccartonii*, *F. gracilis* etc.) are even hardy enough to withstand our winters out of doors, too. Plants may be

Sutton's Charm chrysanthemums
(what a greenhouse full!)

Above left: Oncidium papillio – The Butterfly Orchid

Above right: Paphiopedilum (Cypripedium) insigne 'Harefield Hall'

Right: Cattleya 'Michaelmas'

Above: Pleione formosana
(syn. *P. pricei*)

Left: Cymbidium 'La
Belle Annabelle' (ring
twice for Anna!)

  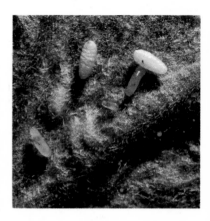

Above left: Green Lacewing fly

Above centre: Adult leaf miner on chrysanthemum leaf

Above right: Larvae and pupae of chrysanthemum leaf miner

Left: Chrysanthemum leaf miner damage

Below left: unsprayed rose afflicted with powdery mildew

Right: similar rose bud but sprayed with 'Benlate' systemic fungicide

Plate 42 Gloxinias in greenhouse

grown on one stem as standards, only allowing the single stem to grow until it has reached the required height, then pinch it out and the top will form a bushy head so long as you do not let the sap from the roots be wasted in stem side shoots – nip them off as they appear. If grown as bushes or for hanging baskets they should have the tips pinched out when they have two to four pairs of leaves, treating the side shoots in the same way. one of my favourites is a far-from-new variety *F. fulgens*, with really striking orange-scarlet flowers. Fuchsias belong to the same botanical family as the Evening Primrose.

Gloxinias

Hothouse tuberous-rooted plants from Brazil with lovely velvety trumpet-shaped flowers ranging in colour through white, pink, red, purple etc. They flower from about midsummer to early autumn and can be grown either from tubers or from seed.

Purchased tubers are started into growth in heat in spring by setting them in seed boxes on a layer of moist peat.

If grown from seed, this should be sown from January to March in a temperature of 15°C to 18°C (60°F to 65°F) in a proprietary seed compost, well moistened, with a little fine silver sand sprinkled over them and a pane of glass placed over the seed pan. They are not covered with paper or kept dark by any other means as gloxinia seeds seem to germinate more freely when exposed to the light. Prick out the seedlings in John Innes Compost No. 1, then pot on in stages until finally they are potted into 5 in. or 6 in. pots containing John Innes Potting Compost No. 2. Grow the seedlings throughout in a temperature of about 15°C (60°F), shading from direct sunlight in the summer months, keeping a fairly humid atmosphere by damping down once a day. (Damping down only means watering the greenhouse floor and paving so that the moisture will evaporate in the hot sunshine and create a degree of humidity in the atmosphere.) In October, gradually reduce the watering and from November keep the plants quite dry so that the soil may be removed from the tubers and they can be stored until the following February or March. They are then restarted into growth on a layer of moist peat in a temperature of 15°C (60°F).

Hydrangea hortensis

These popular pot plants are best renewed annually from cuttings, although older plants can be grown in large pots or tubs containing John Innes Potting Compost No. 2 (lime-free compost for blue-varieties) to which a little extra peat is added. If blue flowers are required, first select a blue variety (this sounds obvious, but even a blue variety can produce mauve flowers if the soil in which it is grown is alkaline), make sure there is no chalk or limestone in the compost, and use a proprietary hydrangea colourant compound according to instructions.

Cuttings can be taken at almost any time during the growing season, but for plants which will flower early the next year take cuttings in March or April from firm non-flowering stems of old plants. Insert the cuttings in sand and peat in the greenhouse with a temperature of 10°C to 15°C (50°F to 60°F). When well rooted, pot singly into 3 in. pots of John Innes Potting Compost No. 1 or peat-based compost.

Water freely and grow on in the greenhouse, with shade from direct sunlight. Artificial heat is not required in the greenhouse from May to October, and plants may even be put into a cold frame from June to September. Pot on into 5 in. pots in John Innes Potting Compost

No. 2 for red varieties or lime-free compost for blue varieties when the 3 in. pots are full of roots, and pinch out the tip of each plant about a fortnight after repotting to encourage branching. Return them to the greenhouse in September and at the same time pot on the largest plants into 6 in. pots in a similar compost.

Water rather sparingly from November until January and maintain a minimum temperature of 7°C (45°F). Then raise the temperature to 10°C to 13°C (50°F to 55°F) and water more freely for early flowers. Of course, do not forget occasional feedings with a liquid fertiliser.

Kalanchoe

Natives of tropical and South Africa and belonging to the crassula family, these attractive succulent plants with brilliantly-coloured scarlet and pink flowers are among my favourite indoor plants. They should be exposed to the maximum amount of direct sunlight and only need a minimum winter temperature of 10°C (50°F). During the summer water must be applied freely, but in winter only sufficient should be given to prevent the stems from shrivelling. Propagate from summer-sown seed or cuttings taken and inserted in a sandy compost in April.

When the plants are repotted or young plants are potted for the first time in spring, firm the compost around the roots but give no water until the soil becomes dry. Start watering after a few weeks and gradually increase as the summer progresses.

Lantana

A greenhouse perennial, growing to a height of about 1½ ft, which belongs to the verbena family. The name 'lantana', is the old name of the viburnum, and if grown from seed the resultant hybrids may produce viburnum-like flowers of lilac, carmine, gold, pink, apricot, salmon or scarlet – a magnificent colour range. It makes a neat pot plant, vigorous and easy to grow, but the seeds (which may be sown at any time of the year) are very erratic and difficult to germinate. I find that if the seeds are soaked in nearly – but not quite – boiling water for about two hours before sowing it helps to break the dormancy. (Of course if the seed is sown as soon as it is ripe it will have a better chance.) Moisten the sowing compost without saturating it and sprinkle the seed very thinly on the top, then gently

Fig. 8 Geranium cuttings

firm the soil. Place them in a heated greenhouse and/or a seed propagator, providing you can maintain the germination temperature of 22°C (72°F), but do not allow the soil surface to dry out. Shortly after germination seedlings should be grown in a cooler temperature of about 13°C (55°F). Transplant gently at the four-leaf stage to their 3½ in. flowering pots, and I find it better to water from the base of the pot with rain-water at greenhouse temperature.

Monstera deliciosa (Swiss cheese plant)
The large green, shiny deeply cut leaves are leathery in texture and perforated with large holes. In its natural habitat it is a climbing plant, clinging to other trees by means of long, cord-like, brown aerial roots developed along the stems. It does have flowers which are yellow and in the form of a spathe, like the arum lily (a member of whose family it is). These may be followed by cylindrical pineapple-like fruits, which are edible and taste like a mixture of pineapple and banana. Of course this does not often happen in the house or greenhouse, because when a monstera is mature enough to produce fruit it is usually about 10 ft. to 15 ft. high. However, there are exceptions to every rule – as the girl said as she tried to strike a match on a wet piece of soap – and you may be lucky. This plant seems to do well in a minimum winter temperature of 13°C (55°F) in a compost of 3 parts turfy loam, 1 part granulated peat, 1 part coarse sand, 1 part well-rotted farmyard manure.

As with *Ficus elastica* and most large-leaved plants, the monstera breathes through the pores in its leaves, which can get clogged up with dust, so they should be sponged with tepid water about three times a week.

If the aerial roots look unsightly, you could either remove them or bury their tips into the soil in the pot if they are near enough. Propagation is by stem cuttings inserted singly in a mixture of equal parts of sand and peat, and put in a propagator at about 21°C (70°F).

Pelargoniums
Pelargonium is the correct botanical name for the greenhouse and summer bedding plants commonly called geraniums. There are numerous types, classified as ivy-leaved, zonal, scented-leaved and regal, and can all be grown in a minimum greenhouse temperature of 10°C (50°F). Cuttings may be taken at almost any time,

but I find September-taken cuttings make the best plants for the following year. Don't forget to leave the cuttings on the staging for three or four hours after taking them so they can dry out and be slightly calloused over before being inserted in the mixture of equal parts of coarse sand and peat. This should reduce the risk of damping off.

Primulas
The two most popular greenhouse varieties are *P. obconica* and *P. malacoides*, because in each case they are fairly easy and very rewarding. *Primula obconica* carries its quite large flowers of blue and pinks in loose heads which it will keep on producing most of the year. (Some people are allergic to this variety, the touch of which can cause quite a skin rash, so make sure they don't affect you.)

Primula malacoides has smaller flowers in larger sprays, the colours ranging from pinks through mauves to crimson. Sow seeds of both varieties in April or May in a temperature of 15°C (60°F) in a moistened proprietary seed compost. *P. obconica* (like gloxinia) seems to germinate best in the light, so cover the seed pan with glass but not with paper. Prick out seedlings into John Innes Potting Compost – first No. 1 and finally No. 2 in

Plate 43   *Monstera deliciosa*

Plate 44 *Primula malacoides*   Plate 45 Potted rose (forced in greenhouse)

5 in. pots – water freely and grow in a cool, well-ventilated greenhouse or frame during the summer months and from October onwards keep in a minimum temperature of 7°C (45°F).

Roses

It is always an interesting experiment to grow roses in a cool greenhouse, and most varieties in bush form may be grown this way. Although not absolutely essential, much better results are obtained if the roses to be forced have been established in their pots for twelve months beforehand. Potted in John Innes Potting Compost No. 3 in 8 in. or 9 in. pots, they should be pruned really hard, left for about three weeks and then taken into a slightly heated greenhouse in November and watered freely. When the flower buds appear, feed every ten days or so with a liquid fertiliser and spray every three or four weeks with a systemic insecticide to keep greenfly at bay. After flowering they are moved

out of doors and the pots plunged in the ground up to their rims (still remembering to water regularly) and in the autumn should either be repotted or generously top dressed with rich soil, some of the old top soil being removed to make room.

Saintpaulias (African violets)

Greenhouse flowering plants which were introduced into this country from Central Africa in 1894. There are varieties with violet, purple, red, pink or white – single or double flowers – which, under the right conditions, are produced almost continuously. They are really attractive little plants with their masses of violet-like flowers nestling on a cushion of velvety dark green oval leaves. These leaves are hairy and must not be wetted or they will rot, so always water from the bottom or, if you are very careful, from underneath the leaves (lifting them) at the top. Grow saintpaulias in a mixture of 1 part peat to 3 parts John Innes Potting Compost No. 1 in 3½ in. pots

Plate 46 *Solanum capsicastrum*

and keep shaded from direct sunshine. They like a minimum temperature of 13 °C (55 °F) and as humid an atmosphere as possible – which is why they prefer the kitchen or bathroom to any other room in the house. Try to remember that they are jungle plants, where the air is hot and humid, and the sunlight hardly ever filters through. Water freely in spring and summer and moderately in autumn and winter. The most popular method of propagation is by leaf stem cuttings. Mature leaves are removed in summer – complete with leaf stalks – and inserted like cuttings (leaf stalk buried to junction of leaf itself) in peat and sand in a propagator with a temperature of 18 °C (65 °F).

Solanum capsicastrum (The winter cherry)
A very popular winter greenhouse plant because of the abundance of cherry-sized orange berries it produces around Christmas time. They are easily grown from seed sown in a warm greenhouse in February or March. Pot up seedlings in John Innes Potting Compost No. 2 and stand them out of doors in a sheltered, sunny place from June to September. Syringe daily with water while the plants are in flower in early summer to help the fruit to set, and feed with a liquid fertiliser from May to August. Of course water freely from April to October. During the winter keep in a greenhouse in full light in a minimum temperature of 7 °C (45 °F).

Plate 47 *Strelitzia reginae*   Plate 48 Streptocarpus

Strelitzia reginae

This is called the Bird of Paradise Flower because its orange and purple flowers bear a striking resemblance to the head of a crested bird. It belongs to the banana family, has large ornamental leaves reaching a height of 3 ft or so, and produces its exotic flowers in spring and summer. It may be grown in 8 in. or 9 in. pots in John Innes Potting Compost No. 2, to which has been added a little extra peat or leafmould. It needs a minimum winter greenhouse temperature of about 13°C (55°F) and during the summer months likes plenty of ventilation in full sunlight. Keep moist in summer, fairly dry in winter. Repot in spring and propagate them by detaching and potting small side shoots or offsets.

Streptocarpus (Cape primrose)

Excellent plants for the cool greenhouse, producing attractive funnel-shaped flowers from spring to autumn. They are usually grown from seed though they can also be increased by leaf cuttings in a propagator in summer. Sow the seed in March in a temperature of 15°C (60°F) and prick out into John Innes Potting Compost No. 1. Water freely and shade from strong sunlight. No artificial heat is required from May to September, but in the autumn a minimum of 13°C (55°F) should be held. Streptocarpus is a member of the gloxinia family and its natural habitat is mainly South Africa.

9 Greenhouse climbers and annuals

Listed here are some of the most beautiful of greenhouse plants – all climbers in their own rights – which can make your greenhouse a showpiece if you can allocate one end to a climber of your choice – or perhaps the wall of a lean-to may be clothed with one. All need support of some kind, either wires or trellis, and most, when young, can be grown around a wire loop in a pot so that it can be moved about as a normal house plant. True climbers may attach themselves by means of tendrils, in which case the supports provided for them must be thin enough for the tendrils to twist around them; they may actually entwine around anything convenient which they touch, such as posts or pillars, or they may cling with suckers or aerial roots to a wall. As a general rule, remember that if you want a plant to grow strongly and healthily it must have sufficient food and water at the times when it is exerting its greatest amount of energy, i.e. during the growing and flowering period. Climbers are, of course, no exception, as they make more growth each year than most other plants. As no roots can take in any fertiliser unless it is completely soluble, it is always better to feed plants with a liquid food.

Be careful when introducing permanent climbers to small greenhouses – all may seem well for the first year while the roots are becoming established, but once the plants have really got going they may grow rapidly, take over half the greenhouse and cut off a great deal of light. The Passion Flowers and jasmines have this tendency and should be kept strictly for the large greenhouse.

Allamanda cathartica

A beautiful evergreen climbing plant which grows wild in tropical America and belongs to the periwinkle family. It is a vigorous climber with large rich yellow trumpet-shaped flowers nestling amid shining green leaves from May to September. It has long trailing shoots which will twist around any available support, and for successful cultivation needs a minimum winter temperature of 13 °C (55 °F). It may be planted in a greenhouse bed or in a 12 in. pot of a compost consisting of 1 part leafmould or peat, 2 parts medium loam and 1 part old and well-rotted farmyard manure. As the shoots develop they are trained on wires attached to the side or roof of the greenhouse. Very little water is required during the winter, but during the summer the compost must be kept moist, with liquid fertiliser applied once every three weeks. Shade from strong, direct sunlight and prune back the previous year's growth in February. Propagation is by 3 in. long cuttings of young shoots taken in March, which root quite quickly in a propagator having a temperature of about 18 °C (65 °F).

Aristolochia elegans (The calico plant)

A warm greenhouse climber from Brazil which, during August and September, produces such a profusion of its curious pale yellow mottled flowers veined with purple as to create quite an outstanding effect. The growths are inclined to be straggly and unless trained to the roof need the adequate support of pillars or trellis. If they are trained to the roof, the growths can be cut back in winter to give light to plants growing beneath. Increase by early summer cuttings in a propagator.

Bougainvillea

Although magnificent specimens of this deciduous climber shrub literally bring alive the holiday villas of Spain, Majorca and Corfu in the summer months with their vivid rosy-red bracts, it was originally discovered in Brazil. The flowers of bougainvilleas are quite insignificant; it is the brightly coloured bracts that provide the display and last for so long.

They can be grown successfully in a minimum winter greenhouse temperature of 10 °C (50 °F) and need no artificial heat from May to September. The best compost consists of two-thirds turfy-loam and one-third peat,

Plate 49   Bougainvillea

sand and broken brick. During the summer months an abundance of water is necessary, but in winter the soil is kept almost dry. In summer give them good ventilation, full sunlight and weekly feeds of a liquid fertiliser. Good drainage is essential wherever you plant – either in a large pot or the greenhouse bed – and as the growths develop they should be tied to wires fixed to the greenhouse roof. Pruning consists of cutting back the lateral shoots of the previous summer's growth to within two buds in March, at the same time removing all weak or overcrowded stems. Increase by inserting cuttings of half-ripe wood, about 4 in. long, in August. As shown in Plate 49 young plants may be grown in 5 in. pots, supported by wires and treated as a house plant.

Campsis radicans (Trumpet vine)

This is a lovely climber from North America, with woody growth furnished with ivy-like aerial roots by which it clings, although additional support is desirable. It has attractive pinnate leaves and in late summer the lateral shoots bear terminal clusters of showy, funnel-shaped flowers of orange and scarlet. It can be grown in a cool greenhouse having a minimum winter temperature of 7°C (45°F), in a large pot or tub of John Innes Potting Compost No. 2 or in a bed of good loamy soil. It is a sun-lover, so do not shade, and needs plenty of water in spring and summer but much less in autumn and winter. To keep it within bounds and encourage flowering, it is sound practice to prune back the lateral growths to two or three buds in autumn, when the leaves have fallen. If you miss then, leave the pruning until the following February or March. Propagation may be by cuttings in early summer or by layering, but sucker growths often provide a ready means of increase.

Cobaea scandens (Cup-and-saucer vine)

Although this is a good fast-growing perennial, it is so easily raised from seed that it is often grown as an annual. The saucer-like green calyx behind each cup-shaped purple flower obviously suggests its common name. It can be grown in any frost-proof greenhouse or even in an unheated greenhouse if the plants are purchased in May and discarded in October. It thrives in any good garden soil, and is best grown from seeds sown thinly in pots of sandy soil in a temperature of about 15°C (60°F) in March, the seedlings being potted singly in small pots of John Innes Potting Compost No. 1 and later moved on into larger pots of John Innes Potting Compost No. 2 or planted in a greenhouse bed of good soil. Water freely in spring and summer, and if the plants are to be carried on as perennials, rather sparingly in autumn and winter. Do not shade. In February or early March, the laterals or side shoots are pinched back to about two buds and all weakly growths removed. An easy climber for the beginner.

Dipladenia

Delightful evergreen climbing plants from Brazil, belonging to the periwinkle family. They have slender, twining stems, smooth oval leaves and bear clusters of rose-pink, purple or white trumpet-shaped flowers

F

Plate 50   *Cobaea scandens*

Plate 51   Ipomoea

throughout the summer. Shade from hot sunshine and keep in a fairly moist atmosphere. During the summer months an abundance of water is required, and the leaves should be frequently syringed to keep down red spider. Liquid fertiliser should be applied to established plants at weekly intervals throughout the growing season, when, of course, plenty of water is needed. From October to March drier conditions may be maintained, but don't allow the soil to stay dry for too long at a time. A minimum winter temperature of 15°C (60°F) is suitable. The growths will need support in the greenhouse, and side shoots may be cut back in February or March. Increase by cuttings of firm young growth in early summer, rooted in a temperature of about 21°C (70°F).

Hoya carnosa (Wax flower)
The flesh-coloured wax-like flowers of this climber are so delightfully beautiful that one can hardly help falling in love with them at first sight. It climbs by means of its thick, succulent stems, clothed in evergreen, oval, fleshy leaves, and bears large clusters of star-shaped flowers in late summer. Each flower has a deeper orange pink centre. It requires a minimum winter temperature of 7°C (45°F) with little watering during this period although it should never be allowed to become dry. Plenty of water in spring and summer, when shade from strong direct sunlight is needed. Train on to wires fixed to the greenhouse wall or roof, and very little pruning is needed as the flowers are borne on the stumps of the previous year's flowering stalks. The leaves and stems should be frequently sprayed with an insecticide to keep down mealy bug. Propagation is by cuttings or layering of firm young shoots in early summer.

Ipomoea (Morning Glory)
This is a family of vigorous climbers with lovely wide funnel-shaped white, blue, rose or purple flowers. As will be readily seen from the character of its flowers and heart-shaped leaves, they are members of the convolvulus family and will cling to any available supports with their twining stems. The flowers of most kinds open early in the morning and although individually they last but a few hours, others are produced in quick succession to keep up the display throughout most of the summer. Do not shade, since they love the

sun. The most popular varieties of ipomoea are easily grown as annuals, seed being sown singly (or in pairs) in small pots of seed compost in March or April in a temperature of about 15°C (60°F). Seed germinates more evenly if soaked in water overnight or lightly chipped before sowing. Grown on in large pots or tubs and trained up a trellis support, they will be quite happy so long as the temperature never falls below 10°C (50°F).

Plate 52 *Hoya carnosa*

Plate 53   Lapageria

Jasmine

There are several beautiful Jasmines available for cultivation in a warm greenhouse where a minimum temperature of 13 °C (55 °F) can be maintained. These include *J. rex*, from Siam, with large white flowers, *J. sambac*, the Arabian jasmine, which bears scented white flowers at almost any time of the year, and *J. grandiflorum*, from the Himalayas, with fragrant flowers of white and rose during late summer.

One of my favourites is the primrose jasmine, *Jasminum primulinum* from China, which has large, often semi-double rich yellow flowers in early spring. It likes a sunny aspect in a frost-proof greenhouse with a minimum temperature of about 7 °C (45 °F). Its long, slender stems can easily be trained on to a wall or trellis.

All these jasmines are best planted in beds of good loamy soil, though they can be grown in large pots or tubs of John Innes Potting Compost No. 2. They should be pruned after flowering as required to keep them within bounds, and all are readily increased by cuttings or layers.

Lapageria rosea (Chilean bellflower)

This strikingly attractive climber, belonging to the lily family, may be found growing wild in Chile. It has wiry, twining stems, rich green oval leaves, and beautiful large bell-shaped pink, white or red flowers with an almost wax-like texture, in summer. It is nearly hardy and can be grown in any frost-proof greenhouse in large pots or tubs containing a lime-free compost made up of 3 parts peat, 1 part medium loam and 1 part silver sand and crushed charcoal. It can also be planted in a greenhouse bed of loam and peat with a sprinkling of a general fertiliser added. In all cases, good drainage is essential. Water freely in spring and summer, moderately in autumn, sparingly in winter and shade from direct sunlight from May to September. It needs the support of trellis or wires, and should be fed with a weak solution of liquid fertiliser once a fortnight from May to August. Very little pruning is normally necessary and propagation is fairly easily effected by layering.

Passiflora caerulea (Passion flower)

As this is quite hardy planted against a sunny wall in some districts, it therefore makes an ideal and easy subject for a cool greenhouse. From the peculiar arrangement of the

various parts of the blooms this plant has been given the name of Passion flower. The flower consists of an outer ring of ten petals, which were thought to represent the ten apostles who actually witnessed the crucifixion of Jesus Christ. Within these, there is a ring of filaments, suggesting the crown of thorns, whilst the five stamens represent the wounds, and the three stigmas the nails. Can be planted in large pots or tubs of John Innes Potting Compost No. 1 but will do better if planted in a bed of good, well-drained loam. Light pruning is carried out as soon as the flowering has finished. This consists of thinning out weakly shoots and regulating the growths so that they fill the allotted space, without overcrowding.

Plate 54   Geranium-covered greenhouse wall

The main branches are secured to wires or a trellis fixed to the greenhouse wall or roof, and the short, lateral shoots are allowed to hang down freely in order to display their attractive blossoms. Increase is by summer cuttings in a propagator, or from seed in a temperature of 18°C (65°F).

Regularly I get letters from friends who have a Passion flower which each year produces an abundance of growth but no flowers, and I usually reply more or less as follows:

'A Passion flower is sometimes a rather tricky plant in so far as its main object in life seems to be to make as much growth as possible and to exert all its energies to this end. If you prune it too hard it will only make more growth, so that isn't the answer. You know, nature is really wonderful – if a plant has to struggle to keep alive and feels that it may die at any time, its immediate reaction is to reproduce itself and let its offspring carry on the line. It does this by producing seeds, which, of course, are prefaced by flowers. As the flowers are necessary to attract the insects which help pollination, it seems that the answer to the problem may be along these lines. In other words, try to restrict the growth of your Passion flower by withholding water and fertiliser other than just sufficient to keep it alive. If the loam is too rich, replace it by a coarse sandy compost, and let's hope you get an acceptable reaction from the plant next year.'

Plumbago capensis

The lovely clusters of pale blue flowers of this climber from South Africa seem to offer a striking contrast to the normal colours of other indoor plants, and if only for that reason it must be a valuable subject for any frost-proof greenhouse. It is suitable for cultivation in tubs or large pots in a greenhouse having a minimum winter temperature of 10°C (50°F). It will do well in John Innes Potting Compost No. 2, or planted in a bed of good soil to which peat and bone meal has been added. Water copiously in spring and summer, but rather sparingly in autumn and winter. It should be grown in full sunlight with plenty of ventilation in summer. The long shoots may be trained on to a trellis fixed to the greenhouse wall, providing the wall is not heavily shaded by other climbing plants trained beneath the roof. Another way of managing *Plumbago*

capensis is to train the shoots on a balloon-shaped or flat trellis fixed in the pot or tub. In March shorten all sideshoots to a few inches and remove weak or overcrowded stems altogether. Then let the greenhouse temperature rise a little, water more freely and restart the plant into growth. It can be increased by cuttings of firm young shoots in early summer, dipped into a rooting hormone powder and set in a propagator.

Pelargonium (Geranium)

Although covered in Chapter 8 as ordinary House Plants, ivy-leafed geraniums are naturally trailing plants which can readily be trained up walls on wires or trellis-work. Some vigorous zonal varieties can also be trained in a similar way, though they will take longer and require a good deal more summer pinching and training to get growth where it is required. However, whatever the trouble and care involved, some of the most colourful greenhouses I have seen were so because of a lovingly-trained geranium-covered wall.

Plate 55   Passiflora (Passion flower)

Plate 56 *Thunbergia alata*

Stephanotis

A beautiful greenhouse climber with waxen pure white scented flowers in summer. It is sometimes called the Clustered Wax Flower because its tubular flowers hang in clusters, and another name given to it is Madagascar jasmine. Water copiously during the summer months, but only moderately in the winter. The foliage should be syringed twice a day from April to September, except when the plant is actually in bloom. A stephanotis needs a minimum winter temperature of 13 °C (55 °F), and should be fed with a liquid fertiliser once a week from May to August. It should also be sprayed with Malathion occasionally in summer to keep down mealy bugs and scale insects. Propagation is by cuttings of short side shoots taken in spring.

Thunbergia alata (Black-eyed Susan)

This is a slender twiner given its common name because each deep orange flower has a black centre. Although actually a perennial, it is usually grown as an annual from seeds sown three to four to a 3 in. pot in John Innes or peat-based seed compost in March in a temperature of 15 °C (60 °F). Pot on seedlings and water copiously to help growth, not forgetting to feed with a weak solution of a liquid fertiliser once a fortnight. It likes sun (so do not shade), and makes a splendid plant for a hanging basket. However, it is at its best when trained on a sunny wall of the greenhouse.

10 Growing tomatoes, cucumbers and out~of~season vegetables

Tomatoes

As I said in Chapter 1, there is nothing quite like the joy of actually picking and eating your own home-grown vegetables, especially those grown out of season and, for my part, this particularly applies to tomatoes. To grow them out of doors in this country is a tricky business, but in the protection of a greenhouse – heated or not – it is amazing how even the most inexperienced of gardeners can get exciting results. Of course there are rules and principles to watch, but these are certainly not complicated, as you will see.

First sow your seed, but before that you will have to select the variety you would like to grow, so here are just a few suggestions:

Ailsa Craig
A good old variety which retains its popularity because of its flavour and reliability.

Big Boy (F1 Hybrid)
Produces very large fleshy fruits. May be grown in a similar manner to normal varieties, except that it is better not to allow more than three trusses per plant owing to the size of the individual fruits.

Eurocross (F1 hybrid)
If you can get the BB strain of this one, all the better, but all are recommended for an early crop in a heated greenhouse. Disease resistant and crops well with large fruits.

Golden Sunrise
You want to be one up on the Joneses and produce golden-yellow tomatoes? Well here's your chance! Nice round medium-sized fruits with a good flavour and a reasonably high yield. Often yellow tomatoes have a noticeably sweeter flavour than most reds.

Moneymaker
A reliable old standby and – like the fox-trot – still as popular as ever. Medium-sized, well-shaped scarlet fruits produced in abundance. Certainly won't let you down.

Sutton's Alicante
Greenback-free, smooth-fruited early variety which is also resistant to Cladosporium disease. Good cropper.

Tigerella
Some novelties are useless except to talk about at the club. Here is a novelty tomato bearing fruits of excellent flavour, which are red with golden stripes when ripe. It ripens early and is free from Greenback.

Ware Cross (F1 Hybrid)
A vigorous grower with fairly large, extremely solid fleshy fruits of particularly good flavour. Ripens early and was bred by the John Innes Institute.

Seed may be sown from January onwards according to the heat you have available. If a minimum temperature of 16°C (60°F) cannot be provided, it is best to wait until March before sowing seed, or to buy tomato plants in pots in April or May.

If you have a heated seed propagator which can provide the above minimum temperature, this will save wasting fuel on heating up the whole of the greenhouse, and you will find that your seeds will germinate in one to two weeks.

Very early seed sowings will produce ripe fruit in a well-heated greenhouse from May onwards, and it is possible to have an autumn crop from an early summer sowing, provided that the plants are in their final positions before the end of July.

Tomatoes are susceptible to many different diseases but some varieties are more resistant than others. However, cleanliness is most important in all pots and seed

Plate 57   Tomato seedling – correct handling by holding a seed leaf

trays, as well as the compost itself, so that the plants are not exposed to any more dangers than is absolutely necessary. John Innes seed compost is quite suitable for sowing tomato seed, although it is quite easy to make up a compost yourself with a mixture of loam, peat and coarse silver sand. It is always advisable to bring the seed compost into the greenhouse a few days before sowing so that it can warm through.

Firm the compost in the seed pans or trays and then sow the seed as thinly as you can. Actually, the seeds are quite large so that you can empty the packet into the palm of one hand and place them in the compost singly with the thumb and forefinger of the other. They are then covered by sieving a ¼ in. layer of the compost over them, and watered thoroughly by standing the pan or tray in a bowl of water at greenhouse temperature. (If they were watered from the top, the seeds would soon be exposed.) A sheet of glass is then placed over each container to prevent too much evaporation, and brown paper laid on top of the glass to provide dark conditions. The glass sheet is turned every day, when the underside is wiped to remove excess moisture, and as soon as signs of germination are seen, the glass and brown paper are removed. The seedlings may be potted into 3 in. pots of John Innes Potting Compost 1 as soon as the first pair of true leaves have formed. Gently holding one of the true leaves (not the stem), ease the seedling out of the compost by lifting with a plant label under the roots, and replant it into the pot as carefully as you would put a new-born baby to bed. Never let the seedlings dry out and keep the atmosphere fairly moist, too. You do not, however, want to force their growth too much since strong, sturdy (and not leggy) specimens are required, but neither do you want any check to continued healthy growth, so you must aim for a happy medium. Keep the minimum temperature of 16°C (60°F) at least until the seedlings have made new growth. See that they have adequate light, and during favourable weather some ventilation should be given for at least half an hour or so at midday. Remember that this is probably mid-winter so stay with them during this exercise. Of course a fan heater should by itself provide sufficient air circulation but a little daily fresh air should be let in too. Let the atmosphere become drier as the seedlings develop so that watering with tepid water should be carefully regulated and not overdone.

Gradually more and more ventilation is given during the day as and when the weather permits, and the minimum temperature slowly lowered to 13°C (55°F). Give the plants more room as they develop and usually they will be in 5 in. pots of John Innes Potting Compost No. 2 within five or six weeks from the time of sowing. Tomatoes may be grown directly in the greenhouse bed (provided the soil is changed or sterilised each year) or in large pots of John Innes Potting Compost No. 3, but I prefer the more modern method of growing them by RING CULTURE.

By this system, the plant develops two sets of roots – one set by which it drinks and one by which it is fed.

Plate 58   Setting out tomato plant alongside bamboo cane

Plate 59   Tomatoes in clay pots in greenhouse

their own way down through the compost into the aggregate searching for moisture. This won't take long as the plant soon gets thirsty.

Now as soon as the first truss of tomatoes has set and the individual fruits are about as big as marbles (and not before, unless you want leggy plants with little fruit), you may start applying a liquid fertiliser to the compost in the ring to be taken up by the other set of roots.

Water is a vital part of the development of the growth of the tomato, and the plant can thus take in all the water it needs unhampered by fertilising salts, and so promote healthier growth and more resistance to disease.

Let me explain . . . Start by making a 6 in. deep bed of washed gravel or clean boiler ashes (which have stood outside for at least a month) on a sheet of black polythene laid over the greenhouse border. Make a few drainage holes in the polythene with a fork, and then water the bed thoroughly. Over this bed, about 1½ ft apart, stand a number of bottomless 9 in. pots or 'rings' filled firmly with John Innes Potting Compost No. 3, and into these carefully plant the now sturdy tomato seedlings, one plant to each ring. The compost in the ring is then given a thorough watering, which is the last time you will actually water the ring, except such as is necessary for applying liquid fertiliser.

From now on you will keep the bed of gravel or ashes well watered to induce the second set of roots to make

Plate 60 Pinching out side shoots of tomato plant

See that you get a proprietary tomato fertiliser with a high potash content, and apply according to the instructions on the bottle. No roots can take in fertilising salts until they are completely soluble, so that is why a liquid fertiliser is to be preferred. Of course no fertiliser must be applied to the drinking roots in the gravel or the whole principle of the system will be broken down.

The tomato has a natural tendency to branch freely but is usually grown with a single stem in the greenhouse. It may be supported by bamboo canes, stakes or plastic-covered wires, but more usually by fillis string tied to overhead wires in the roof and sometimes to horizontal wires near to the ground. I say 'sometimes' because the ground wires are not always used and the fillis string hanging from the roof is just twisted around the young plant which then proceeds to grow around and up to the string, obtaining all the support it needs.

Persistently pinch out all side shoots arising from the leaf-axils (the angle between the main stem and the leaf stalk), and 'stop' the main stem when five or six trusses have developed.

Provide some light shade in periods of hot sun, and remember that overhead syringeing of the flowers with water from a fine mist spray encourages a good set of fruit. Alternatively, the trusses may be 'set' artificially with a proprietary fruit-setting hormone solution based on a growth-regulating substance. Such a solution often promotes fruit development largely without seeds, and is useful in ensuring a full set of bottom or top trusses and of winter crops, when natural conditions may be against fertilisation. The solution should only be applied once to each truss, preferably when all the flowers have developed. No attempt should be made to save seed from plants thus treated.

Fig. 9   Tomato ring culture

Plate 61   Tomatoes – blossom-end rot

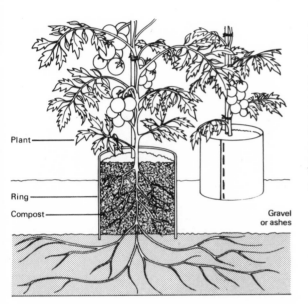

Plant

Ring

Compost

Gravel
or ashes

dark areas on the leaves. If the attack is only slight, the plants may be grown on, encouraged by good culture – if it is severe, however, the plants should be destroyed. Another type of *Mosaic* shows up as bright yellow patches on the leaves, and infected plants should be pulled up and burned, renewing the soil and spraying with a copper-based fungicide before any more tomato plants are put in. So you see, the road to successful tomato culture can provide a fascinating journey with a pot of gold at the end of it. If you are not already an addict give it a try – to a gardener of the right calibre the mere challenge will appeal, and the first fruits of his first s ccess will make him a king in his own home!

Plenty of good airy ventilation should be achieved without allowing the tomato plants to catch cold. To get air circulation without draughts, and to refresh the atmosphere without undue chilling needs plenty of care on windy, cold or wintry days. Roof vents should only be opened on the lee side on windy days. Ventilation should be increased with the warmth of the day, and ceased in the evening in order to conserve the warmth accumulated within the greenhouse. As I said before, tomatoes are susceptible to many ailments, but we will look at this problem more fully in Chapter 15. However, most of these will be avoided if we provide the right growing conditions.

Poor circulation of air coupled with too much warm humidity can be the cause of *botyritis, tomato blight, rust,* etc., whilst lack of or inconsistent watering may cause *blossom-end rot* or *fruit cracking. Greenback* (which has been mentioned before and is shown by the area around the stalk not colouring properly) is the result of either too little potash or too much sun, and then there is *dry set* (when the flowers do not drop off but the fruits remain tiny and undeveloped) which is due to faulty pollination from too dry an atmosphere. One serious virus disease is *Mosaic* which may be seen as a mottling of light and

Cucumbers

It is not advisable to grow cucumbers and tomatoes in the same greenhouse at the same time, as the former require much more humidity than would be healthy for the latter. Cucumbers need a minimum temperature of 16°C (60°F) for successful cultivation. The exception is when the seeds are sown (edgeways in John Innes Seed Compost) between February and April, a minimum temperature of 18°C (65°F) then being required. Sow one seed to a 3 in. pot of John Innes Seed Compost.

Mounds of soil about 10 in. deep by 2 ft across are built on the staging of the greenhouse, with one cucumber planted in the apex of each. The mounds should be hotbeds consisting of a shovelful of stable manure covered by a 6 in. layer of fibrous loam – old rotted turf loam is ideal. Having watered them in well, each plant

is attached to a cane tied to wires stretched 9 in. apart
horizontally along the greenhouse roof about 1 ft from
the glass. As the leader and side shoots develop they are
tied to the wires with fillis string. The main growth is
allowed to reach the apex of the greenhouse before
stopping, but all side growths below the bottom wire
are removed and the growing points of all other side
growths are pinched out at the second leaf. As the blooms
appear, pinch out the smaller male flowers leaving the
female flowers, which may be recognised by the small
bulbous swelling (which is the start of the fruit)
immediately behind the flower.

Cucumbers are surface-rooting and fresh compost
may be added to the mounds when the roots appear
through the soil. Ventilate freely in warm weather and
syringe the plants once or twice every day with tepid
water. Maintain a moist, warm atmosphere and close the
vents early in the afternoon.

Plate 64   Cucumbers in greenhouse

Fig. 10   Pot-forcing chicory

Plants set out during the last week in May in an unheated greenhouse and given the above treatment should produce cucumbers in late summer and early autumn.

Three reliable varieties are 'Telegraph' (one of the most popular and a heavy cropper), 'Conqueror' (dark green, long shapely fruits) and 'Butchers Disease Resisting' (a heavy cropper which is immune to leaf spot disease).

Chicory

This is grown for the sake of its blanched, leafy shoots, which may be obtained in winter by forcing the roots into premature growth in warmth. Plants lifted from the open ground from October onwards may be forced in a greenhouse with a minimum temperature of 9°C (48°F). Dry off the roots for a day or so immediately after lifting so that they receive a temporary check to growth. Prepare them for forcing by cutting off all top growth to within an inch of the crown, shorten the roots to about 8 in. with a sharp knife or secateurs, and reject all fanged (double rooted) specimens.

Where small quantities are concerned and space is limited, three or four may be planted in 9 in. or 10 in. pots of pebble-free sandy loam, and a similar-sized

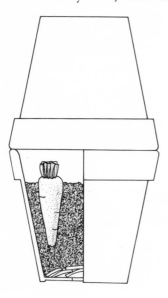

pot inverted on top. This ensures the darkness which will blanch the shoots.

For larger quantities the roots may be planted similarly in deep, covered boxes. Heavy soil, bad drainage and heat above 15°C (60°F) are things to avoid.

To start, seed may be sown out of doors in May in light loamy soil; before the seedlings become too crowded, thin them out to about 9 in. apart.

Mint

I love to pick fresh mint during the winter, and this presents no problem if you have a greenhouse where a temperature of 10°C (50°F) can be maintained. It can be grown in seed trays, boxes, large pots or even in the greenhouse border – but here, without restriction, it may spread too rapidly and too far. If possible, start the mint in September/October under cool conditions, and bring it into the warm greenhouse as soon as you see any sign of new growth. When growing nicely, a few fine mist sprays of 'aired' water will provide the atmosphere liked by these plants, and it should be possible to cut shoots over a long period.

Lettuce

Seed can be sown from August and September onwards, the earliest sowings being ready somewhere about December, with October sowings maturing about February. If you want lettuce to cut in March, sow seed at the end of October, putting the plants in their final positions in December. For a heated greenhouse one of the most reliable varieties is 'Cheshunt Early Giant', but if this is not available try 'Cannington Forcing'. Sow in seed trays, later pricking out into other boxes of John Innes Potting Compost No. 2. Seed may also, of course, be sown in the greenhouse border – as outside. A suitable seed-sowing temperature is 14°C to 16°C (56°F to 60°F), this being lowered to about 10°C (50°F) after germination. Watch out for the grey mould fungus, *Botrytis cinerea*, which often attacks lettuce under glass if they are overwatered. If you see any sign of it, dig up and destroy the affected plants immediately. It may be recognised by the grey masses of spores on the surface of the affected leaves, and sometimes the plant topples over or even breaks off. It is therefore essential to avoid excessive watering, undue splashing of the leaves and fluctuations of temperature.

Plate 65   Rhubarb may be easily forced under the green-house staging

Dwarf French Beans

Very welcome crops of dwarf French beans, of a variety like 'Improved Canadian Wonder' or 'The Prince', may be grown in pots in a heated greenhouse from seeds – sown at intervals from September to February. Well crocked 10 in. pots are filled three-parts full of John Innes Potting Compost No. 2. Space seven or eight beans over the compost and cover them with a 1½ in. layer of soil. Keep the pots in the greenhouse in a temperature of 15°C (60°F), and as the beans germinate reduce them to five to each pot. At first water is given sparingly, then freely as growth advances. Lightly syringe the plants at frequent intervals – this not only helps the flowers to set well but keeps down red spider. When the plants are about 8 in. high the soil is top dressed to within 1½ in. of the top of the pots with more John Innes Potting Compost No. 2. Once the pods have set, apply liquid manure at ten-day intervals, and for support a few twiggy sticks are placed in the pots. The aim should be to maintain a temperature of 13°C (55°F) or so, although no harm is done if it rises a little during the daytime. They appreciate fresh air but not draughts, and are really most tasty out of season.

Rhubarb

Three-year-old crowns are best for forcing in the green-house. These should be lifted outside in November/ December and left on the surface of the ground for a couple of weeks to expose them to the air and a few night's frost. (It is most interesting but true that many plants actually react more favourably to forcing if they are first of all retarded by either cold or dryness.) The roots, with the crown exposed, are then planted in deep boxes or in the ground below the staging. The light is excluded by hanging a mat or thick hessian down from the staging (front and back if your greenhouse is glass-to-ground), and the plants are then ready to produce early and tender fruit. Give a light watering in a temperature of about 7°C (45°F), but after a couple of weeks this may be increased to 13°C (55°F). Don't allow the temperature to get much higher than this or the sticks will become flabby. Sticks should be ready for pulling in about five or six weeks. Most varieties of rhubarb may be forced, but naturally the earlier kinds are best – 'Prince Albert' matures most quickly, if you have any choice.

Mustard and Cress

These are so easy to grow they hardly need be mentioned, but I will, if only as a reminder. The seed can be sown in boxes, pots, in the greenhouse soil or even – as a novelty for the children – on a damp flannel. Sow little and often, as they do not last long. Water the seed compost well, and when the surface moisture has drained off a little, sow the seed fairly thickly, lightly pressing it in. There is no need to cover the seeds with soil, but if you lay a piece of cardboard over the box or pot to provide darkness, the cress will germinate in about a week and the mustard in three to four days. Obviously then, the cress should be sown about three or four days before the mustard, so that they mature together.

Plate 66. Strawberries in pots – fruits on a greenhouse-grown plant

Strawberries

To force plants under glass, strong runners (which have been layered in July or August) should be selected, kept well watered and syringed in dry weather. They should be potted on into 5 in. or 6 in. pots about a month after severance from the parent plants, or when their roots are filling the smaller 3 in. pots. A good compost is a mixture of 3 parts (by bulk) good loam, 1 part well-rotted stable manure, ½ part sharp silver sand plus 4 oz hoof and horn meal per bushel.

The potted plants should be stood on a layer of ashes out of doors, and kept watered and syringed in dry weather until late November. By that time the plants will have become dormant and should then be laid, in their pots on their sides, and covered with straw or peat as a protection against frost. In late December or early January, the pots of strawberries should be taken into a cool greenhouse and watered if dry. Until growth begins afresh only sufficient heat to maintain a temperature of 7°C (45°F) is necessary for the first month. Flower trusses should begin to show in February, and the heat should be increased to a minimum temperature of 10°C (50°F). The atmosphere should be kept moist by syringeing, and ventilation maintained without draughts. When the plants are in flower, they should be pollinated with a rabbit's tail or soft camel-hair brush, and the atmosphere may be allowed to become a little drier. After petal-fall it is a good idea to thin the fruits to not more than seven or eight per plant, re-moisten the atmosphere by syringeing, and water and feed with a liquid fertiliser to swell the fruit. The strawberries should be ripe and ready for picking by mid-April or May – a month or so after flowering. One final sad note . . . after giving you such wonderful rewards, the plants should be discarded when they have fruited.

Plate 67   Group of cacti

11   Cacti, succulents and hydroponics

It is said that to sit on a Prickly Pear is a sign of an early spring, but let's not jump to conclusions regarding the popularity or otherwise of the cactus family. To some they hold an almost hypnotic fascination, and yet a challenge, as a beautiful yet dangerous snake. To others the main appeal of the members of this family is their lethargic demand for so very little of one's time and energy. The real cactus lover, however, sees them for what they are: beautiful bastions of nature, equipped so efficiently to withstand conditions of arid, heat-ridden starvation which no other genus of plant life could survive, and yet to celebrate their annual short-lived refreshment and relief from dryness they will produce flowers of breath-taking beauty and colour. This is partly what makes them so unique and their culture so fascinating that many cacti societies have been formed throughout the world.

The members of the cactus family exhibit a great diversity of form, some are small and resemble pebbles in shape and colouring, others form columns 20 ft in height. Some are armed with sharp, pointed spines and all have a thick outer skin. The absence of leaves and the thick skin enable these plants to flourish in dry, barren climates where other vegetation could not exist because transpiration (losing moisture by evaporation etc.) is reduced to an absolute minimum. During the often-too-short rainy season cacti have that camel-like quality of being able to store up large quantities of food and water, which is slowly released during the subsequent long periods of drought. In addition to being curiously attractive in form as we said, many cacti also bear brilliant flowers of many beautiful shades. Some are even night-flowering as, for example, the large white fragrant *Selenicereus grandi-florous*, a climbing cactus from Texas where it is sometimes called 'Queen of the Night'. Cacti and succulents are to be found in America, South Africa and many other parts of the world where the climate is dry and arid for most of the year and the rainfall very sparse and almost inconsequential. Though commonly described as desert

plants, cacti cannot survive without water in some form or other, and are to be found only in those places which do get rain, however intermittently.

In the cultivation of each individual variety of cactus, try to learn and bear in mind the climatic conditions prevailing in its natural habitat, and if you can reproduce even some of them you will be well on your way to success. Cacti and succulents are grouped together because they emanate from, and therefore require, similar growing conditions. One of the main differences between them is that succulents are without spines, and that is why very often the non-addicted prefers them to cacti. The family are also very accommodating as regards greenhouse temperatures – many of them can be grown where there is a minimum winter temperature of 7°C (45°F), and yet so long as there is ample ventilation 21°C (70°F) or more during the summer will not harm them. It is sometimes said that cacti, being desert plants, need very little water. This is only partly true, for in their natural habitat they are subjected to long spells of dry weather followed by periods of abundant rain. It is then that the plants make new growth, extend their roots and store the water in their swollen stems, living on this reserve throughout the next dry period. It is this capacity for storing water that has given rise to the stories of travellers and desert beasts quenching their thirst by drinking the sap produced after pulping the tissues of the cacti. Actually, the moisture is generally very bitter, most unpalatable and would be almost as distasteful as sea water. However, I think if I were dying of thirst in a desert and came across a pachycereus the taste of the sap wouldn't put me off!

A number of cactus species can withstand quite cold conditions providing the air is dry and the soil is well drained. High up on the rocky slopes of the Andes mountains may be found species of columnar cacti, where very low temperatures and even snow are endured during the short winter months without causing much harm to the plants.

Although cacti flowers are very short-lived, they attract bees or other insects for pollination by their scent or by their brilliant colours. Under the right cultivation most species will provide blossoms when the right state of maturity is reached, and continue to do so year after year. The flowering size depends upon the species, for such plants as mammillaria, rebutia, epiphyllum and lobivia will bloom when only one or two years old from seed, whilst the larger cereus may have to be much older before doing so.

The spines, which replace the non-existent leaves on most cacti, have uses other than that of protection from grazing animals. They provide a certain amount of shade from the sun, and attract and concentrate moisture from the air during the night, causing the water to run down the ribs of the plant to the ground where the roots are waiting. At the base of the spines are 'areoles', from which grow small bristles or woolly tufts. Areoles are special organs which are the source of all branches, roots, flowers, leaves, joints or spines. As they have no leaves, transpiration and respiration are undertaken by the stems of cacti which are green with chlorophyll. This is the reason why many species are covered with a white powdery substance, which fills up the pores and prevents excessive transpiration loss of moisture during the long hot days. On the new growth, where this covering has not yet developed, cacti produce woolly masses as protection to the tender parts. I only mention these points to give you an insight as to their survival and success.

Although succulents, other than cacti, depend for their attraction to a great extent upon the wonderfully varied colours of the leaves they also produce flowers of brilliant beauty and form. Amongst the most colourful of the succulents are the mesembryanthemums from South Africa. These plants bear flowers of every vivid hue, and include the very curious and interesting species called 'living stones' or lithops. Of course not all succulents are tender, the race includes such common rock garden plants as sedum (stonecrop) and sempervivum (houseleek) both of which sport the distinctive fleshy leaves.

Since they are able to survive without water for quite long periods, cacti and succulents can be very convenient plants for gardeners who have to be away from home a great deal or when short holidays are taken. Always remember, however, to give abundant water prior to your departure and on your return.

For greenhouse cultivation most cacti require a minimum temperature of 4°C (40°F), and even the more tender of the succulents are quite content with a minimum of 10°C (50°F) provided they are kept fairly dry in winter. They must, of course, be exposed to all the available sunlight throughout the year, although the zygocactus, epiphyllums and their allies prefer a little bit of shade in midsummer. If it is found to be necessary, repotting is best done in April in a special cactus compost or one consisting of a mixture of 2 parts sandy loam, 1 part leafmould and 1 part fine (⅛ in. down) grit with a little charcoal added. Always fill about one quarter of the pot with drainage crocks beneath the compost. Keep the compost reasonably moist for the first three months,

Plate 68 *Aporocactus flagelliformis*

then for the remainder of the summer less water is given and the plants are exposed as fully as possible to air and light to ensure the production of flowers. From October through to April very little water is required, sufficient only being given at about monthly intervals to keep the stems from shrivelling. They, of course, need occasional feeds of liquid manure throughout the summer.

Cacti may be propagated from seed, or you will find that pieces of stem or shoot, taken from any part of the plant, will form roots. When cacti produce offsets, these form a ready means of increase. They need only be carefully removed and potted up when of a reasonable size and they will soon form roots.

When cacti cuttings are taken, lay them on a shelf or staging in the direct sunlight for a day to two to allow a corky skin to form over the cuts, which prevents rotting. They are then inserted in a sandy compost and placed on the greenhouse staging.

Cacti and succulents are not, as a rule, greatly troubled by pests or diseases. One pest which may attack the plants above or below ground is the *mealy bug*, a tiny bug-like creature protected by a covering of a white waxy substance. If you see it on the plant, carefully pick it off with a pointed stick or spray with an insecticide called Malathion, which will also kill off scale insects.

From the vast number of species available, here are just a few easy ones which are suitable for greenhouse culture.

Cacti

Aporocactus flagelliformis
This has the unfortunate common name of rat-tailed cactus, but produces brilliant red flowers in early spring.

Mammillaria
Smallish and neat, they freely produce each year flowers of cream, yellow and carmine.

Opuntia
Well-known cacti with flat pads, oval joints or cylindrical stems. The flowers are mostly red and if you are lucky they may be followed by edible berries which taste a bit like gooseberries.

Plate 69   Mammillaria

Top:
Plate 70   *Echinocactus grusonii* (The Golden Ball Cactus, which provides sap to drink for thirsty travellers in the desert)

Bottom:
Plate 71   *Echinopsis multiplex*

Echinocactus (The Hedgehog Cactus)
Round masses of tissue with conspicuous longitudinal ridges with spines and densely woolly at the top. Mature plants bear yellow flowers in summer. Easily grown from seed.

Echinopsis
Similar to echinocactus, bearing pink, white or yellow flowers in summer.

Epiphyllum
Leaf-flowering cactus from Brazil, where they grow chiefly on trunks of trees, have short wood stems and flat, fleshy, pendant branches divided into sections. They make excellent subjects for growing in baskets suspended from the greenhouse roof. Flowers vary from white to yellow and pink through to bright red. Easily propagated from cuttings.

Succulents
Agave
Sometimes called the Century Plant because they grow so slowly. After producing the tall branched spikes of flowers, most of the agaves die, though suckers may develop at their base. Even if this does not happen the flowers will have dropped their seeds. In the greenhouse they need a rich porous soil and large pots, and should be given full sunlight and a free circulation of air.

Kalanchoe
As a succulent it makes such a good house or greenhouse plant that I included it in Chapter 8.

Mesembryanthemum
The name that calls to mind the tender annuals which provide such dazzling displays of colour on the rockery, in the border or at the seaside throughout the summer months. The 'ice-plant', too, is a mesembryanthemum, and another member of the family is the lithops or 'living stones'. However, this is a large and interesting family, most species of which make excellent greenhouse plants with a wide range of flower forms and colours.

Crassula
This genus contains a large number of species, mostly from South Africa, producing red, orange and yellowish

Plate 72   Epiphyllum

Plate 73 Kalanchoe   Plate 74 *Echeveria retusa*

flowers among fleshy leaves. Easily increased from cuttings.

Echeveria
Members of the crassula family with lush, fleshy foliage usually covered with an attractive dusting of white mealy powder, giving it a lovely glaucous effect. They have small tubular-shaped flowers of bright red, orange-yellow or greenish-pink, and can very easily be increased by removing small leaflets and simply pressing them into a sandy compost. There are about 100 species of echeveria but one of the most popular is *Echeveria retusa* which grows about 18 in., with fleshy, glaucous leaves and stems terminating in clusters of orange-coloured flowers. It makes an excellent house plant.

Sedum
Many stonecrops are very hardy, but some are tender and make good house plants. *Sedum sieboldii* has the blue-grey leaves with rosy-mauve flower heads in September/October, and *Sedum morganianum* carries its silvery-green leaves in long tassels. Both may be grown in pots or suspended from a hanging basket in the greenhouse or outside.

Zygocactus truncatus (Christmas cactus)
This showy succulent of the cactus family is a native of Brazil, and is now known by the uncomfortable name of *Schlumbergera buckleyi*. (Currency was changed to decimal for national and international convenience, I sometimes wonder whether the changing of botanical names is

just a fashionable ploy of the theorists.) It has flattened jointed stems, gracefully arching, and these are terminated from December to February by drooping scarlet – or even white – flowers, lasting several days. It is an epiphytic cactus, i.e. one which receives much of its food from the air, and during the summer months likes to be placed in a semi-shaded spot where it gets a full circulation of air. It thrives in a compost consisting of grit and loam, and, unlike most cacti, appreciates plenty of water while in active growth. It is quite easy to propagate by inserting the flattened stems into a sandy compost and keeping reasonably moist in a temperature of about $15°C$ ($60°F$).

Hydroponics

Hydroponics is the art and science of growing plants without soil by means of nutrient chemical solutions.

The practice consists of growing plants in a suitable rooting medium which gives the roots access to balanced and aerated nutrient solutions, in the presence of adequate sunlight. While commercially most successful in sunny climes, on barren lands where fresh produce has scarcity value, and for out-of-season or highly-priced flowers or vegetables, the technique is adaptable for gardening pleasure, profit and experiment. The hydroponic system can be used where soil culture is impossible – in towns, flats, flat house roofs, etc.

The advantages claimed are much higher yields and uniformity of growth, virtual freedom from weeds, greater resistance to disease, and savings in time and labour in looking after the plants during growth. Incidentally, there is no discernible difference between the hydroponic-grown produce and the naturally grown in flavour, vitamin or nutrient-content.

In earlier experiments, plants grew in a seed bed consisting of litter (wood-wool, peat straw, etc.) laid on a wire mesh, suspended over a tank containing a nutrient solution, with an air space between the seed-bed and the solution. The roots of the plants grew down and drew nutriment from the solution. Later, the technique of circulating nutrient solutions through inert rooting substances – sand, gravel, vermiculite – was found to give better results, and is now more generally employed.

In Great Britain, hydroponics is best adapted for greenhouse use. Tanks or troughs can be made from a variety of materials – metal, wood, concrete etc.; or window boxes and plant pots can be used. Zinc or galvanised metal, however, should be avoided, unless painted over with bitumen, as zinc in excess is often toxic to plants. Tanks can be built for permanence, *in situ*, or be portable. Dimensions should be about those used for growing plants in soil.

The tanks must be constructed to drain easily. This is simply arranged with small tanks by sloping them slightly to one end with a drainage outlet. Larger tanks are usually made with a camber at the bottom, with drainage holes at every 15 in. at the sides, outletting to drainage channels which collect the surplus solution. Ready-constructed tanks in small sizes for the back-yard or town gardener are available on the market.

The Rooting Medium. Various aggregates are used for the rooting medium. A depth of at least 6 in. is desirable with the container filled to within 1 in. or $1\frac{1}{2}$ in. of the top. Fine gravel, $\frac{1}{8}$ in. to $\frac{3}{8}$ in. crushed stone, cinders, broken brick, or granite chips, with a proportion of sand, may be used. Sand alone is good; preferably a neutral lime-free sand, such as red, silver or white sand, coarse in texture and washed. For the gardener, one of the most useful materials is Vermiculite, a micaceous mineral, which holds moisture well and is sterile and light.

Two Methods of Feeding are practised: surface-watering, and sub-irrigation. Simple surface watering, using a sand culture, consists of regular watering with a watering can or hosepipe, using an appropriate nutrient solution. This system works satisfactorily with pots or small containers. For sustained feeding, automatic overhead spraying of the sand beds with a dilute nutrient solution is used commercially. An alternative is to allow the dilute solution to drip-feed continuously from a tank through a feed line, the surplus solution being collected in a sump and pumped back to the reservoir. Another modification is to apply dry mixed nutrient salts periodically and water them in.

In sub-irrigation, the tank is periodically flooded with dilute solution from below, then allowed to drain. The drained solution is collected and re-used. By means of a pump, the system can be made automatic, but the solution needs periodical renewal. The solution enters the beds through short lengths of plastic tubing when the bed is extensive.

Ideally, the composition of the nutrient solution should be calculated to suit the plant species to be grown

Plate 75   Crassula

Plate 76 *Zygocactus truncatus*

Plate 77 Cacti grown by hydroculture

and the conditions under which it is grown.

Here is a formula for a popular nutrient solution:

60 g ammonium sulphate	
114 g potassium monobasic phosphate	Dissolved in
280 g magnesium sulphate	100 gal of
972 g calcium nitrate.	water.

Alternatively a balanced nutrient can be bought already prepared for dilution, in compound or tablet form.

The acid-alkaline balance of pH of these solutions is important. For most plants, the solution should have a pH of 6·0. If it is greater than this, it should be adjusted by adding dilute sulphuric acid (3 parts acid, 7 parts water). For roses, a pH of 6·0 to 7·0 is in order. For carnations, the pH may be 5·0 to 6·5. Rain or soft spring water is best for these solutions, but where a hard water containing lime, must be used, particular care must be taken to correct the pH to the desired value.

In theory, any plant that can be grown by ordinary methods and soil culture can also be reared by hydroponics. In practice, however, the gardener will probably find it best to grow those plants which best repay him for his trouble. Most vegetables can be grown, including salad vegetables such as lettuce, radish, young onions, celery, endive, and produce such as tomatoes, sweet corn, potatoes, carrots, leeks etc., yield excellently. Peas, beans and other legumes mature satisfactorily. Most flowers, particularly annuals, grow well, and the system is admirable for carnations, roses, gardenias, etc. Out-of-season produce needs atmospheric heat and the same care as when grown in soil culture.

Small seeds are best raised separately in pans or boxes, using Vermiculite or John Innes seed compost, and the seedling transplanted to the beds with as little disturbance of the roots as possible. Large seeds such as those of peas, beans, sweet corn, etc., are best placed direct in the aggregate. Bulbs should be placed up to their shoulders.

Seeds germinate quite readily under hydroponic conditions, and plant growth is more rapid and sustained, than in soil culture. Plant tissues do tend to be softer and less hardened, and therefore supports, in the form of canes, wires and fillis, will be needed for the taller-growing plants. Otherwise, cultivation should follow normal horticultural practice.

12 Chrysanthemums and carnations

Chrysanthemums

For those who lean towards, or like to specialise in one species of plants, the chrysanthemum is an ideal subject on which to lavish one's detailed care and attention, producing, as it does, such magnificent and spectacular blooms in a comparatively short time. Local as well as national autumn flower shows invariably include one or more chrysanthemum classes in their schedules, so that even the greenest amateur, if he or she grows blooms of which to be justifiably proud, may compete with better known and more experienced growers and even carry off prizes. Of course, one must learn how to display the blooms to their best advantage at a show, and to that end there are many local chrysanthemum societies, as well as, of course, the National Chrysanthemum Society, you could join to get expert advice.

The flowering times of chrysanthemums are controlled partly by lengths of daylight and darkness and partly by temperature variation. It is possible to control both to a great extent by special artificial daylight lighting and, of course, temperature, and so produce plants and flowers throughout the year. As you know from seeing in florists' shops the apparently dwarfed chrysanthemums in pots, commercial growers do exactly that, but for the private gardener it is usually more convenient to allow the seasons to take their natural course and to grow greenhouse chrysanthemums to flower from October to January. There are a great many varieties which are classified according to the shape and size of their blooms, and to whether they are naturally early flowering (August-September), October flowering or late flowering (November-January). It is only the 'Octobers' and 'lates' which need to be flowered in the greenhouse, but all classes are usually over-wintered in a frost-proof house, increased in a cool greenhouse and grown on with frost protection at least until May. Not only must they be protected from frost but also, in winter, from excessive moisture which can do them as much harm. From late May or early June until towards the end of September all chrysanthemums are better out of doors than under glass. Consequently the chrysanthemum grower can have his greenhouse free throughout the summer for a crop of tomatoes, a bonus of which many take advantage.

There are different methods of culture (including even ring culture), but the best plants are still those grown in pots throughout, thus making them more transportable and avoiding any check which occurs when roots are disturbed. For propagation the usual procedure is to prepare cuttings between February and April from young shoots about 3 in. long, growing from the roots of old plants which have been cut back hard after flowering and kept reasonably moist in a temperature of 7°C to 10°C (45°F to 50°F). Each cutting is cleanly severed just below a joint, the lower leaves removed and the base moistened and dipped into a proprietary hormone rooting powder. The cuttings are then inserted into a mixture of equal parts of coarse sand, loam and peat around the edges of half pots or in shallow seed trays. They should be rooted either in a propagator or on the open staging of the greenhouse, in which case they will need rather more watering and overhead mist spraying to prevent flagging. An air temperature of 10°C (50°F) should be maintained for speedy and successful results. When they are rooted the cuttings should be potted into 3 in. pots of John Innes Potting Compost No. 2 or peat-based potting compost, and grown on in a cool greenhouse (temperature about 7°C (45°F)), shading for the first few days then allowing all the light they can get.

As soon as the small pots are full of roots the plants should be moved into 5 in. pots, and a few weeks later their final move to 8 in. or 10 in. pots should be made. Always pot firmly – finger pressure on the compost down the sides of the larger pots, followed by two or three sharp taps with the bottom of the pot on the bench, usually works the soil in well. A good tool here, however, is a blunt-ended piece of wood which can be used as a rammer to ram the new soil around the sides of the pot. Always finish the compost 2 in. or 3 in. below the rim of the pot to allow for watering and top dressing as the season advances. At this stage each plant should be provided with a strong 4 ft cane for support. Meanwhile the growing tip should be pinched out when it is about 8 in. high, and the tips of side growths similarly removed when they are a further 8 in. or 9 in. long. This is called 'stopping', and encourages the plants to branch out from low down the stem, but it is not always a good policy to retain all the branches that result. You cannot altogether control the amount of growth sap coming up from the roots, but you can control its distribution. If you leave only, say, three branches on a plant the resultant three blooms will each be twice as large as they would have been if you had left six branches on the same plant. So you see, the number of branches you retain will depend on the kind of flowers required. For very large exhibition blooms three stems to each plant may be ample. At the other end of the scale, for

a big display of small flowers, a dozen or more branches may be left. However many stems are retained, each should be tied individually to the supporting cane to prevent breakage. Very large plants may require several canes angled to lean outwards at the top to allow for the spread of the stems. The dates of 'stopping' are not always vital unless you are growing plants for exhibiting on a particular date, but if this is the case you will usually find that the catalogues of chrysanthemum specialist nurseries give the instructions required for each variety. The end of May or early June is a good time for the October and November flowerers, while the December varieties can be 'stopped' about the middle of April and again in June. If any of the November-flowering plants are particularly advanced in growth, they could be stopped in April and then again in June. Unwanted side shoots must be constantly removed, tying checked regularly and a constant watch kept for insect pests or possible diseases.

When all risks of frosts is past (May/June) the potted plants should be stood outdoors without cover but in a sunny place where they are not likely to be damaged by winds. Stand the pots on a gravel or cinder base and tie the support canes to wires stretched horizontally between posts driven in at either end of the row of pots.

Throughout their growing season chrysanthemums should be watered freely, each time giving a thorough soaking.

From about mid-June until the first petal colour is seen, plants should be fed every week with a special proprietary liquid chrysanthemum fertiliser. To strengthen the root system, and build up really strong plants, top dressing with compost is necessary. (Remember 2 in. or 3 in. was left between the top of the compost and the pot rim specifically for this.) This may be done three times at fortnightly intervals commencing mid-July with John Innes Potting Compost No. 3, or a mixture of turf loam, peat and well-rotted farmyard manure. After top dressing, the rose should be used on the can when water is given to avoid making holes in the compost. When the flower buds start to appear you must decide whether you want one large bloom on each stem or a cluster of smaller ones. If the former, pinch out all but the terminal bud at an early stage; if the latter is required pinch out the terminal bud only and leave the rest. This is called 'disbudding'.

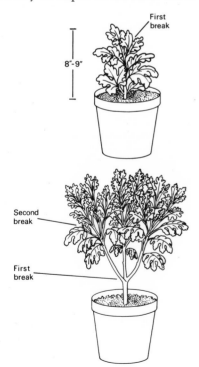

First break

8″–9″

Second break

First break

Fig. 13   Disbudding chrysanthemums

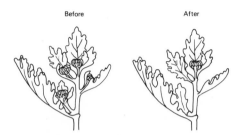

Before   After

In September (long before night frosts restart) all plants are returned to the greenhouse and grown in maximum light and a temperature of 10°C to 15°C (50°F to 60°F). Free ventilation is allowed so long as the plants do not suffer from draughts or too much variation of temperature. Some heat may be required not only to maintain the minimum temperature but to dry the atmosphere and prevent decay in the opening blooms. After flowering, stems are cut down and pots kept frost-free until it is time to restart growth to provide the next season's cuttings.

'Charm' and 'Cascade' chrysanthemums make delightful pot plants for room decoration. Introduced by Suttons in 1933, they form compact dome-shaped or looser and more informally-shaped plants massed with literally hundreds of small single flowers in pastel shades of pink, yellow, red and bronze. All have a faint but distinct violet-like fragrance, and may be raised by sowing seed in gentle heat, 10°C (50°F), in mid-February. They are then treated as ordinary late-flowering chrysanthemums, except that the final pots need not exceed 8 in. Stopping treatment consists solely of pinching out the growing tips when the plants are 9 in. high – they break so freely that further stopping is unnecessary. The stems are strong, dwarf and wiry, and support canes are not required.

The above applies to both Charms and Cascades, but the latter are slightly different in so far as they can also be increased by cuttings, especially if you want to repeat the same colours. Cascades also need special training to achieve a drooping or weeping effect, although they may be grown fanwise or as dwarf 'umbrella' standards. If you want the drooping type, stand the pots during the summer on a tall shelf erected in the garden, say against the sunny wall of the potting shed and at least 4 ft from the ground. Restrict the growing stems to

one or two, which are tied as they lengthen to canes inserted in the ground leaning towards the shelf at a steep angle. To prevent the stems from being broken, they should be gradually turned towards the canes by a loop of raffia and then tied every few inches as growth proceeds. Don't actually remove any side shoots, but keep pinching them back to promote as large a number of buds as possible. At the end of September the ties are released and it will be found that the stems will retain the trained position and make beautiful decorations for pedestals or balconies.

Charm and Cascade chrysanthemums, which are grown from seed, are usually discarded after flowering, unless you want to take cuttings. Do try these beauties, but remember that where Charms are compact, Cascades need more space.

The main flower type divisions for chrysanthemums are as follows:

Single
Up to five rows of petals and a button-like central disc.

Incurved
Petals curling inwards to form a ball-like flower.

Intermediate
Inner petals curling inwards and outer petals curling outwards.

Reflexed
All petals curling outwards.

Anemone-centred
Like single but with a low cushion of very short (usually tubular) petals in place of a central disc.

Rayonnante
Petals rolled lengthwise like thin quills.

Charm
An abundance of small single flowers (often scented) on a bushy plant.

Cascade
Similar to Charm but with a looser habit.

As far as varieties are concerned, it would be presumptuous of me to attempt to make a comprehensive list as new improved varieties (superseding older ones) are constantly being introduced. Write to a specialist grower for a catalogue, or, as I suggested before, join the National Chrysanthemum Society – both will keep you up to date with current trends.

When considering chrysanthemum troubles from pests and diseases, the emphasis should always be on preventative rather than curative measures. Your chances of success could be ruined unless a regular routine system of spraying is adopted. Healthy, well-grown plants are always best to withstand attacks from any source.

Chrysanthemums are not often troubled by serious diseases, but insect pests are liable to cause concern at any time during the season. Use a liquid spray containing a systemic or other insecticide (make sure it is recommended for chrysanthemums) once a week, slightly increasing its strength during the summer months when the pests are most active. During dull, damp weather a systemic fungicide should be included in the spray mixture to prevent an attack of foliar disease. Keep a sharp look-out for leaf-miner, greenfly, eelworm and mildew, but we'll talk more about those in Chapter 15.

Carnations
All plants under this heading belong to the dianthus family, and although various kinds can be grown in the greenhouse, by far the most popular are the incomparable Perpetual-flowering carnations. Wonderful colours, heady scent of cloves, almost continuous production of blooms – rewards such as these automatically support the theory that carnations are difficult to grow. This, of course, is not true provided we remember that they like lime, good open loamy soil with proper drainage, fresh circulated air, full sunlight and freedom from pests. Coupled with the fact that they are quite happy in a minimum temperature of 10°C (50°F), none of the needs are difficult to meet.

To start a collection of Perpetual-flowering carnations. it is always best to buy plants already growing in 3 in, pots from a specialist grower. They will be in the right growing medium, established, healthy young plants which in all probability will have been 'stopped' and will already have one or two sturdy 'breaks'.

For best results, carnations should be grown in a greenhouse alone, and not with other kinds of plants. Make sure they never get pot-bound, moving them from the 3 in. to the 5 in. pots and then on to larger ones according to growth. Always use pots which have been cleaned and sterilised, making sure they are dry.

Avoid potting composts containing peat, which is liable to turn acid as it decomposes, and lime-loving carnations would not be happy if this happened. A suitable growing compost consists of 4 parts (by bulk) good loam, 1 part old farmyard manure, and ¼ part mortar rubble or limestone chippings. A substitute for the farmyard manure – if you can't get it – is 2 parts bonemeal, 2 parts hoof and horn meal, and 1 part dried blood, but as this is a bit more potent than the manure be careful not to overdo it. There are also, of course, special proprietary carnation fertilisers available.

Left and centre:
Fig. 15   Disbudding perpetual-flowering carnations

Right:
Fig. 16   To encourage the growth of flowering shoots near the base of a perpetual-flowering carnation, snap off about 3 in. of the growing point

Carnations like firm potting, but not so firm as to prevent water passing through the compost. Plants intended for winter flowering should be in their flowering pots by the end of June. At that time they can stand on a bed of ashes outdoors, provided they have some shelter from winds and heavy rains. This will lead to well ripened, mature stems capable of producing good quality blooms.

Give thorough soakings of water when necessary avoiding very wet or very dry root conditions at all times. Overhead weekly mist sprays are beneficial and help to keep down pests.

When they are 6 in. to 8 in. high and well established, every young plant should be 'stopped'. If this is done early in the day when growth is brittle, the stem will snap off easily at the joint. The shoot should be broken back into the firm wood – merely pinching out the tip is not sufficient. A second stopping is usually given to the longest shoots formed from the result of the first stop, but this is best spread over a few weeks so as not to cause a check to the plant and to secure flowers over a longer period. As we said before, 'stopping' is simply removing the top of the growth to induce it to produce 'breaks' or side shoots, and so build up good shapely plants. If a plant is not 'stopped' at all, it will probably make long, straggly growth with one flower at the top.

It is best to carry out your programme of 'stopping' between February and August, allowing for resultant growths to mature before winter. As a rough guide, it should take about five months from the time a shoot is 'stopped' until the 'break' produces a flower. Perpetual-flowering carnations in the greenhouse need plenty of support from an early age. Bamboo canes and raffia or rings are often used if you only have a few plants, but for a larger number of plants a good idea is to stretch two horizontal layers of plastic netting at about 1 ft and 2 ft above soil level, so that the carnations can grow up through them for support.

Don't leave the plants out of doors later than about mid-August as it is better that flower buds should form under the protection of glass. From mid-September onwards an occasional weak liquid feed will prove beneficial. Winter blooms are very valuable – not only to your prestige but also your pocket – so watch that the greenhouse heat is not greatly increased, as high temperatures during dull winter weather are detrimental.

Some disbudding may be necessary, but you must choose whether you want fewer larger blooms or more smaller ones on the same plant.

Perpetual-flowering carnations may be propagated by cuttings taken at any time between October and March, though the three mid-winter months are probably most favoured as the most vigorous and hardy plants are obtained from cuttings taken then. Growths selected for cuttings should be 3 in. to 4 in. long and taken halfway up the stem, where it is fairly thick with short inter-nodes. These should be taken by cutting just below a leaf joint or node with a sharp knife, trimming off the lower leaves and inserting them in a sandy compost in a propagating frame the temperature of which is about 13° C (55°F). Pot on into 3 in. pots when seen to be rooted. Use azobenzene smoke bombs in the greenhouse if you see any sign of thrips or red spider, and keep watch for fusarium wilt and rust disease which healthy plants and good cultivation should avoid.

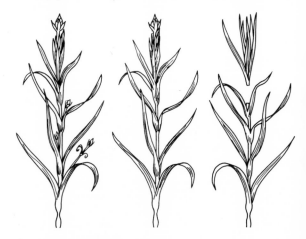

13 Orchids

To the average gardener, orchid growing is a hobby surrounded by an aura of mystique and still reserved for the select few who can afford special houses, special treatment and almost unlimited financial resources. This is as wrong as saying today that golf is a sport enjoyed only by the financially independent upper classes. In each case the expertise and general level of knowledge of the subject has been raised as the cost to each participant has been lowered, with the result that ultimate standards and pleasure of achievement have benefited and been made available to all who are genuinely interested. So please don't be put off by the ill-founded belief that orchids are difficult to grow – some such as the cymbidiums, which we shall discuss later, are amongst the easiest and most inexpensive of greenhouse plants, needing little more than a frost-free house and a few grains of common sense.

There are, of course, some exotic and very choice species which do require special conditions, but there are also many that can be grown along with other plants in a mixed greenhouse and it is on a few of these easy ones we will concentrate later. If at a later stage you become intoxicated with the joy of growing orchids, you can then aim to achieve success with those needing special care.

Many orchids have thickened stems, known as pseudobulbs, which enable them to store food and moisture; consequently they can rest for quite long periods. Some are epiphytic, growing wild on trees and rocks and getting their food from the air and from decayed leaves and other vegetation; but terrestrial orchids root and feed in the soil in the ordinary way. Because of these unusual methods of growing and feeding, most orchids need composts which are different from those used for other greenhouse plants, and their management and culture can vary too. This does not mean that they are difficult to grow, in fact most orchid enthusiasts insist that they are among the easiest of greenhouse plants to manage, being able to withstand a great deal of ill-treatment. Once an understanding or affinity with them is acquired you will be surprised at the new refreshing outlook to growing that will be opened up to you. A gardener who has been accustomed to handling other greenhouse plants must learn new ways when embarking on orchid cultivation. Since many of the plants of this great and numerous family will be growing in spongy mixtures of sphagnum moss, osmunda fibre, leafmould, etc., you must learn to assess soil moisture more by the appearance of the leaves than by the feel of the compost, which would never become waterlogged as it is so open and spongy. Neither do they dry out as rapidly as ordinary pot plants since the atmosphere orchids like is usually humid anyway. If at all possible, only use rain-water at greenhouse temperature.

One important aspect of orchid-growing, which will come with advice, and experience, is in identifying the resting season which is a characteristic of many orchids with pseudobulbs (and of other house plants, too, of course) so that they may be kept sufficiently dry during this period of their annual cycle.

If you start with the few easier-to-grow species listed hereunder, I will try and give you a fair idea as to their seasonal growth pattern, a knowledge of which is essential before you can determine the time of their resting period. As with us and with all living creatures, resting time is so important to health, because it is then that energy is restored, 'batteries recharged' and one is made ready to face the immediate, and perhaps hectic, future. But of course the time will come when you will want to progress to the more difficult species, and as there are literally thousands of orchid species and hybrids known in cultivation today I would suggest that you then get one of the numerous excellent books devoted exclusively to their cultivation.

There is also The Orchid Society of Great Britain, the R.H.S. Orchid Committee and many active local Orchid societies which publish very helpful literature on the subject and enable members to exchange information.

Plate 78   Camplex Humidifier

Obviously I am only able to lightly touch on the subject here, but I hope the touch will be sufficient to whet your appetite and stimulate an interest in a part of horticulture which I think gives perhaps the greatest return in pleasure and satisfaction for the least outlay in time and energy. If finance is a consideration, you have only to start selling your orchid flowers to see that monetary returns aren't bad either. Orchid seed is dust-like and produced in great quantities, but in nature much of the seed never germinates and vast numbers of seedlings die young. Modern technology makes it possible to germinate seeds in test tubes or flasks on a special kind of jelly called agar, impregnated with a nutrient solution and from which all harmful germs are excluded, so that a high percentage of the seed grows and the seedlings survive. Consequently there has been a great increase in available orchid hybrids, and unflowered seedlings of quite good parentage can often be purchased at reasonable cost. But hybrids usually differ from their parents, and while an unflowered seedling may turn out to be better, similar, or even worse than its parents, the purchase of youngsters must be looked upon as a gamble. Even so, I would always advise the beginner to purchase these seedlings rather than attempt to germinate seeds.

Of course, as we have said before, vegetative propagation (i.e. by division or cuttings) always reproduces exactly the full characteristics of the parent plants. A fairly new scientific system of taking minute cuttings from the growing tips of orchid plants and starting them off in slowly revolving flasks containing a nutrient solution, has made it possible to increase selected plants far more rapidly. These are called meristem cuttings and although they must be dearer than the unflowered seedlings they are still comparatively reasonably priced and can be grown on to flowering size in a few years.

Most greenhouse orchids need an equable temperature, a moist atmosphere and shade from direct sunshine in spring and summer. Don't move them around as you would other pot plants, and as good drainage is essential it is wise to stand the plants on inverted plant pots on a staging covered with gravel or ashes. When the temperature goes above about 18°C (65°F) orchids like top ventilation in preference to the greenhouse door being left open. As it is so important, I will repeat that draughts *must be avoided at all costs.*

Rollblinds, which could be pulled up or down according to the weather conditions, provide the ideal method of greenhouse shading, but other types of shading, which may be less expensive and quite effective, may be persevered with.

One essential to successful orchid growing is a humid atmosphere during spring and summer. It may be necessary to damp down the plants, floor and staging more than once during hot sunny days, but this should never be done late in the day or unwanted heavy moisture may remain on the plants through the cooler night hours. Water the plants, if possible, with rain-water at greenhouse temperature.

As an alternative to the above method, there is a product on the market called a Humidifier, which is a pump-type evaporative unit designed for use in greenhouses up to 2000 cubic feet, where it will provide up to 60 per cent R.H. and is self-controlling. In smaller greenhouses it may be desirable to fit a separate humidistat.

Established plants should be watered fairly freely while they are in growth, moderately for a few weeks after repotting, and sparingly during their rest period. As a rough guide, from May to September plants should be given a thorough soaking about every five days. Do not immerse the pot in the water as this would expel the air from the compost and literally 'drown' the plant. Keep some sphagnum moss on top of the compost in the pots, and while it remains green the plants have sufficient moisture, but once it becomes a greyish colour water is needed. Experience will teach you that this method of assessment is not infallible, but it can act as a guide to begin with. *Never give orchids more water when the compost is wet.* This is a fairly obvious statement, but it is sometimes done 'so that they will last a little longer without attention'.

If the orchid is king of the greenhouse it certainly demands allegiance, but nevertheless, if plants are given a thorough soaking and extra damp moss is placed on and around the pots, most of them are unlikely to suffer much harm if left for up to ten days. This is a comfort if you are going on holiday, and don't want to burden a friend or neighbour with the responsibility of a daily plant inspection.

Orchids can be grown in any adequately heated greenhouse, but one with solid walls is preferable to one with glass to ground.

Although they are remarkably free from pests and diseases, it is a good idea to sponge the leaves about once a month with a mild solution of tepid water and insecticide. If you buy plants from a specialist orchid grower it is rarely necessary to repot for twelve months or so. When you do have to repot, use a clay pot which should be at least a quarter filled with crocks (broken pot) for drainage. Ordinary potting composts should not be used for orchids. Special mixtures based on osmunda fibre and sphagnum moss are made up and the exact constituents of these mixtures will often depend on the ingredients available and the species being grown. If in any doubt, I should buy a compost made up by an orchid specialist – then you will be sure of getting the right thing. Charcoal, coarse silver sand, leafmould, peat, bracken, pine bark are all ingredients used in various mixtures. Then put in the plant, working the new compost in between the roots and around the neck, ramming it gently but firmly to keep the plant in position. Never repot into a pot more than an inch or so larger than the previous one. When repotting old plants remove most of the old compost and then divide the plant, keeping three or four pseudobulbs and a new growth to be potted on, discarding the rest. As they grow, the epiphytic species will push roots out over the side of the pot or develop them in mid-air from stems or pseudobulbs. This is quite natural and should not be interfered

with. Most orchids only need repotting every second or third year, but cypripediums may need repotting annually. Never be afraid of letting plants grow large – it is a fact that too frequent division often reduces the number of flowers.

Although some specialist growers have their own ideas on feeding – some even not believing in feeding at all – I feel that orchids can be helped by giving very weak feeds of diluted dried blood or perhaps even bonemeal once a month from April to the end of September. At least one very knowledgeable orchid specialist advocates watering the greenhouse floor and staging early on summer evenings with a weak solution of cow manure, so that the leaves will absorb sufficient from the atmosphere. This is instead of giving a liquid fertiliser direct to the plants, and applies mainly to cymbidiums and cypripediums.

Anyway, here are a few words on some of the easier-to-grow species of orchid:

Cymbidiums

A group of terrestrial orchids which has become increasingly popular owing to the production of a great number of beautiful varieties, their long flowering season and the ease with which they can be grown. This is really the orchid for the amateur. They have conical pseudobulbs 2 in. to 6 in. high with long, strap-like evergreen leaves, and produce arching spikes of bloom from the base of the bulb in the winter and early spring months.

Cymbidiums are very accommodating and seem able to withstand quite alarming fluctuations in temperature, but I would suggest you try and maintain a minimum winter night temperature of 7°C (45°F) which would automatically rise slightly higher during the day. Actually, if the greenhouse is kept at a temperature and atmosphere which you yourself find comfortable, the plants will thrive. No artificial heat is required, of course, from May to September. They are strong-rooted and should be repotted, if necessary, in spring after the flower spikes have been removed, or when young growths are seen. See that all dead and decaying roots are cut away and plenty of drainage is placed in the bottom of the pot. Don't be afraid of cutting the roots, the thick heavy bulbs will keep the plants going for quite a time if necessary. For compost, use 1 part of loam fibre, 1 part of

Plate 79 Cymbidiums at Bell Park 1964

osmunda fibre and 1 part sphagnum moss; more osmunda if the loam is on the heavy side, or even crushed brick may be incorporated to keep the compost open. If you find the osmunda fibre difficult to get, try the following mixture to which a friend of mine introduced me, and which I have found most successful:

1 part (by bulk)	Bracken (Dried)	
1 ,, ,, ,,	Pine bark	all
1 ,, ,, ,,	Sphagnum moss	crushed up
,, ,, ,,	Oak leaves (and/or beech)	and rubbed through
1 ,, ,, ,,	Lumpy peat (from small blocks)	the hands

To every 2 gallon bucketful of the above compost add a 3½ in. potful of charcoal.

This compost is found to keep sweet for much longer than compost involving loam.

After repotting do not water for three or four days, but keep the foliage syringed and the tops of the pots dampened slightly.

The atmosphere must be kept moist and the greenhouse ventilated freely in suitable weather, but draughts must not be allowed. There is no clear-cut resting season, and so water must be given throughout the year, though less is needed in winter than in summer. They enjoy light but not direct strong sunlight, so do provide shading in bright sunny weather. Although the flower spikes

Plate 80   *Cymbidium carica* 'Chelsea'

Fig. 17   Scale insects

are developed in the autumn, the flowers themselves will not normally develop until after Christmas. They will then last two months or more in bloom. To obtain specimen plants, cut the spikes after they have been open for two or three weeks – they will last quite a long time in water.

They are liable to attacks from scale insects, which find a home in the sheathed bases of the leaves around the bulbs and can only be dislodged by careful sponging. Cymbidiums are sometimes (not often) affected by a virus which would appear to be inherent in some hybrids. One of the causes could be cold dank conditions, and I understand excessive manuring could be another, but usually extra warmth will grow them out of it.

Cypripediums

Popularly called Lady's Slipper Orchids from the shape of the slipper-like pouch of the flower which is much used in buttonholes and corsages, and whose colour range takes in almost every shade except blue, Cypripediums are yet another easy-to-grow species. Although the greenhouse varieties are correctly known botanically as paphiopedilum few amateur orchid growers will ever think of them as anything but cypripediums. Their cultural details are much as for cymbidiums – the need for humidity, shading, ventilation etc. are similar, but the cypripedium is, however, a softer growing plant and therefore will not withstand the extremes that cymbidiums will. Shading should be applied a little earlier in the year and retained a little later. The compost should have a larger percentage of osmunda fibre and sphagnum moss, and rather more crocks should be used for drainage as cypripediums just will not tolerate a sodden compost. If the greenhouse temperature can be maintained at between 15°C and 18°C (60°F and 65°F repotting may be carried out in the winter after the flowers have been cut, but failing that, repot annually in April.

Cypripediums have no pseudobulbs and therefore no way of storing food and water within themselves, as the cymbidium. Water must be given them as required, and the compost never allowed to dry out. Neither, of course, should the compost ever be allowed to become waterlogged. If this should happen, put the plant on a shelf immediately, to dry out. Do not cut the flowers until they have been open for at least a week. It is best

to take the advice of your supplier as to what you can grow, and this will depend upon what growing facilities you have available, but *Cypripedium insigne* with its many hybrids, can always be relied upon not to let you down. For all cypripediums, avoid a draughty arid atmosphere in the greenhouse. Don't risk losing humidity by opening the vents too much, but try to keep an even balance of each requirement, whilst watching the temperature at the same time.

Thrips, scale insects and red spider are the chief pests to watch out for, especially if too much heat has been used in summer.

Cattleyas

A large and very varied group of beautiful evergreen Orchids, with large flowers of mauve, crimson-and-yellow or magenta-rose which cut well and are used extensively in corsages. They grow well in intermediate house conditions, with a minimum winter temperature of 13°C (55°F), and require only light shading throughout the summer. They also need more air and light in the autumn to induce the ripening of the summer growths which will help in later production of flowers.

Cattleyas may be watered freely from March to September, always allowing the compost to become almost dry before watering again, but then gradually decrease the frequency of watering and in winter give only sufficient to prevent the shrivelling of the pseudo-bulbs.

During the warm weather growing season overhead mist sprayings are very beneficial.

The standard potting mixture for cattleyas is usually 3 parts dried osmunda fibre to 1 part sphagnum moss,

Plate 81 *Cattleya alba* 'Enid'

chopped finely for seedlings but used in a coarser condition for older plants. Many cattleyas fail through loose potting so make sure that your compost is well firmed in the pot. Repotting should be done as infrequently as possible – only when the old compost has become sour, or if the plant has grown too large for its pot or basket.

Calanthes

Most calanthes are terrestrial orchids which flower in mid-winter. I remember seeing one variety *Calanthe vestita* growing wild in Malaya during one of my wartime visits there. This is a variety which produces shining white flowers on spikes up to 2 ft long during its resting period between September and February. There are many varieties of calanthe with the same timetable, and it is in February that they are repotted in a mixture of 3 parts fibrous loam, 1 part leafmould or peat, ½ part chopped sphagnum moss and ½ part coarse sand. The pots must first of all be one quarter filled with crocks for drainage, over which is placed a 1 in. layer of dried cow manure. A minimum temperature of 15 °C (60°F) must be maintained, especially while the bulbs are being repotted. If there is more than one pseudobulb – and there are usually two – repot them separately and increase your stock. The pseudobulbs must not be buried, but the

Plate 82 *Dendrobium nobile* 'Virginale'

soil brought up to their base, with, if necessary, short sticks to support them. There is a tendency for the roots to raise the bulbs slightly, so this should be allowed for in potting.

Watering at this time must be carried out with great care, for if the new compost becomes sodden, root action is prevented. When the pots are full of roots, however, water may be given freely, and fortnightly doses of weak liquid manure benefit them. Do not syringe the plants in case water lodges in the folds of the leaves.

In the autumn the leaves will begin to turn yellow and the plants will not require such frequent waterings even though the flower spikes will be seen to be developing. When the flowers open fully, the plant will be at rest and watering may be discontinued completely.

When in full growth calanthes enjoy abundant heat and a moist atmosphere. Shading is required, but not heavy.

Dendrobiums

In the same kind of compost and conditions as the cattleya you can grow dendrobiums, and the beautiful small-growing variety *D. agreggatum* will produce a mass of lovely yellow blooms at a time when flowers are not very plentiful. Although a compost of equal parts osmunda fibre and sphagnum moss is usual, some people even grow dendrobiums in nothing but sphagnum moss, and I must say I am surprised to hear they are successful with it, too. A most useful favourite of this family is *Dendrobium nobile* which has stem-like pseudobulbs, and produces its flowers in early spring from the nodes of the previous year's pseudobulbs. The white flowers, tipped with rosy-purple, are comparatively large.

D. nobile is one of the cooler-growing dendrobiums which come from the Burmese end of the Himalayas, and which will stand a resting temperature of as low as 7°C (45°F) in the winter.

Dendrobiums should be planted into as small a pot as will just comfortably take the roots, so that you can be more liberal with the water during the growing season.

The more tender hard-bulbed species are much more difficult to grow, requiring as much light as possible throughout the year and a minimum winter temperature of 15°C (60°F), so to start with I think I should stick to the cooler ones.

Odontoglossums

Most kinds of this important group of orchids have beautiful flowers on long arching scapes. In such a large group as this slightly different treatment must be meted out to the various kinds, but generally all odontoglossums are hill plants and do not require a high temperature. They need a greenhouse with a cool, moist atmosphere and a temperature as near 15°C (60°F) as possible throughout the year. The temperature will, of course, rise during the summer and decrease during the winter, but it must not fall below 10°C (50°F). Ventilation, damping and shading are necessary during hot weather to keep the greenhouse cool and moist – at the same time avoiding draughts at all costs.

Using a compost of 2 parts osmunda fibre, 1 part sphagnum moss, 1 part oak or beech leaves and ½ part coarse sand, repotting should be done in September or early spring. As long as the compost keeps sweet, it need not be done every year. Avoid repotting in the very warm or very cold months, but it can be done whenever fresh growth is seen. Never water odontoglossums or damp down the greenhouse when the temperature drops below 10°C (50°F). Syringe overhead with a mist spray regularly on warm days, but try not to let moisture remain on the foliage overnight. Watch out for thrips and spray as necessary.

Two of the most popular types are:

(1) *Odontoglossum crispum*, which carries its lovely 3 in. white flowers in slender arching sprays and is excellent as a cut flower, needs intermediate house temperatures – min. 13°C (55°F).

(2) *Odontoglossum grande*, however, will grow in a cool house and carries its large yellow and cinnamon-brown flowers in smaller spikes, usually in threes. It is an easy orchid to grow, provided it is given a good rest with very little water in winter. *Odontoglossum crispum* on the other hand, has a less marked resting period,

needs very careful watering at all times, and it and its hybrids are not the easiest of orchids to grow well.

Oncidiums

This large and varied group are all epiphytal and ever-green. They are closely allied to the odontoglossums and should be treated similarly. They also are hill plants and will withstand a minimum winter temperature of 10°C (50°F). Repot when young growths appear from February to April.

Oncidiums usually have small yellow or yellow and brown flowers produced in large branched sprays, but some have larger flowers produced successively, one or two at a time, for most of the year. One of these *Oncidium papillio*, known as the Butterfly Orchid because of the shape of its flowers, requires warm house conditions.

Miltonias

Epiphytal orchids which grow wild chiefly in Brazil and Central America, and which have comparatively small, smooth pseudobulbs set closely together or at intervals on the rhizomes. The flower spikes are produced from the base of the bulbs, and usually bear several pansy-like flowers each. They flower in spring and early summer and grow well in cool house conditions providing the temperature does not fall below 13°C (55°F) at any time. They enjoy a fair amount of shade in spring and summer and a humid atmosphere, so should be watered throughout the year, though less frequently in winter than in summer. They should be repotted annually in a compost consisting of 3 parts cut osmunda fibre, 1 part sphagnum moss, with a quarter part of oak or beech leaves and a little coarse sand and crushed charcoal. Repotting may be carried out in early April or early September.

Pleiones

Sometimes called the Indian Crocus, these orchids are epiphytal or semi-terrestrial, many growing wild in Northern India on banks or tree trunks. Most of them are deciduous and form small fleshy pseudobulbs which are of annual duration only. Most kinds bloom in winter, and as they grow perfectly well in coolhouse conditions, I have always grown them in the Alpine House. They are inexpensive, easy to grow, require very little room,

Plate 83   *Vanda rothschildiana*

yet produce beautiful large flowers of lilac and white. *Pleione formosana* (syn. *P. pricei* – no relation!) has individual flowers about 2¼ in. in diameter, and this is the one I have always found so easy to grow. Divide and repot after flowering in a compost of 1 part chopped osmunda fibre, 1 part loam fibre, ½ part sphagnum moss with some coarse sand and leafmould. In the orchid house they make good stage-mates with odontoglossums.

Vandas

These upright-growing orchids are almost continuously in growth. *Vanda caerulea* is a very distinctive species, with wide sprays of pale blue flowers produced regularly each autumn. For its winter resting period it requires a minimum temperature of 10°C (50°F) and in summer likes to feel the sun (if it's not too strong) on its back so needs only light shading. Water moderately at all times, allowing the compost to get nearly dry before wetting it thoroughly again. Repot only every two or three years, but top dress annually with compost. A refreshing break in orchid colour.

Sophronitis

Hung up and wrapped in osmunda fibre and sphagnum moss, and wired around and on to a piece of bark until well-rooted, *Sophronitis grandiflora* 'Coccinea' will grow

into a perfectly lovely miniature orchid with delightful rich red flowers. This is a really worthwhile orchid to grow and will be quite happy in the same greenhouse as the cattleyas and dendrobiums.

14 The grape vine

The grape vine, *Vitis vinifera*, was introduced to Britain some 1900 years ago during the early days of the Christian era. It came from the temperate regions of the Mediterranean and southern Europe which is the native home of the vine. Although it is usual in this country to plant vines in a warm greenhouse, excellent grapes can be successfully grown in an unheated one, and in warmer districts certain varieties will ripen good quality fruit when grown on a sunny wall out of doors. Also, in sheltered well-drained areas near to water, vineyards in England have been producing wine-making grapes for some time. Whichever way they are grown, success depends on well-prepared fertile soil, healthy plants of reliable varieties, simple pruning and training and plenty of direct sunlight.

Any well-built greenhouse, so situated that there is full access to plenty of sun and light, and provided with good ventilators, is suitable to grow a vine. Apart from a few varieties or when forced early fruit is required, artificial heating is not essential for the production of good grapes. In fact there are several excellent varieties which can be grown to perfection in an unheated greenhouse, especially if it is devoted solely to the production of grapes. Other plants may be grown in the greenhouse provided that, where temperatures, humidity, ventilation, etc. are concerned the vine receives first consideration at all times.

The usual practice is to plant the vine in a prepared border, provided the soil is loamy and fertile, with some well-rotted manure worked in. Good drainage is also important – vines will not grow well where there is waterlogging at any time. The roots of the vine may be planted inside or outside the greenhouse, the former if the greenhouse is heated or the latter if it is unheated. If outside, the vine stem is taken in through a hole in the brickwork or side wall. Whether it is planted inside or out, the soil should contain a certain amount of lime, which can be sprinkled over the surface at about $\frac{1}{2}$ lb per square yard. If the soil is heavy clay, drainage can be improved by digging in coarse sand or gravel as well as organic matter such as peat or leafmould.

Bone meal, at the rate of 1 lb per square yard, forked into the soil will help to supply the nitrogen, phosphate and potash the vine will need. A mulching of about 3 in. of a mixture of manure, peat and loam each year around the roots is also a good idea, but more about that later.

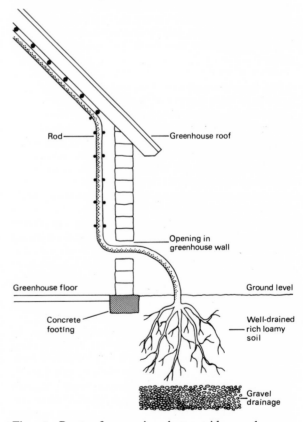

Rod
Greenhouse roof
Opening in greenhouse wall
Greenhouse floor
Ground level
Concrete footing
Well-drained rich loamy soil
Gravel drainage

Fig. 18 Roots of grape vine plant outside greenhouse

As vines are normally grown in pots or containers they can be transplanted from these at any time of the year. However, if you have a choice, September, October, or November is preferred. The reason for early autumn planting is that the plants are pruned at that time so as to avoid damage from bleeding which sometimes takes place when pruning is carried out in winter or early spring.

Soil in the border and around the plant should be comfortably moist before planting, and see that the roots are only set in the soil to the depth at which they were originally grown in the container or pot. Planting too deeply can cause trouble later on. Plant the vines about 5 ft apart if you are growing them on the single stem or rod system, which, generally speaking, is the best way for the amateur to grow vines. If they are to be grown on the extension system, with several stems trained to cover the greenhouse roof, they should be planted at least 10 ft apart.

When planting, dig the hole wide enough to take the roots spread to their fullest extent, and see that it is at least 18 in. from the wall of the greenhouse.

In the spring following planting young shoots will develop. When these have made five or six leaves, remove the growing tip from all except the leading one which will form the main stem or rod, and all sub-laterals (i.e. side shoots off the side shoots) should be pinched out above the first leaf. This treatment should be continued during the summer months, but when the leading shoot has grown about 6 ft, the growing tip should be pinched out and all side shoots stopped above the first leaf, except the top one which will then be allowed to grow on during the summer. Should this shoot grow more than 6 ft another cane can be tied to the cross wires which have been fixed to the beams along the length of the house to carry any extension of the growth of the rod. A well-grown young vine may reach the roof of the greenhouse by the end of the first summer.

In the first early winter after planting, when the leaves have fallen in November, the new rod or leading shoot should be pruned back to 3 ft or 4 ft from the base, and any laterals or side-shoots cut back to two buds to encourage the formation of fruiting spurs. In each succeeding year keep cutting back all side shoots to two buds and shortening the leading young growths to about 2 ft from the start of their growth the previous spring.

During the winter no heat is necessary or even desirable, as this may cause bleeding of the vine by encouraging the sap to flow.

The vine's dormant period is a good time to clean thoroughly through the greenhouse, wiping down all glass supports with a mild disinfectant solution and taking out and burning all leaves, prunings and general rubbish. At the same time refix or extend to vine supports on the greenhouse roof. In a heated greenhouse, vines can be started into growth in February with a temperature of 7°C (45°F), raising this after about a month to 16° (60°F). If the temperature on a sunny day looks like going above 18°C (65°F) open the ventilators to keep it down. Starting this early in the year will, of course, produce early fruit. If your vine is growing in an unheated greenhouse, it should not be started into growth until March or April, and the grapes will ripen in August or September according to variety. The buds on the vine must be encouraged to start into growth evenly, all along the stem, by watering and syringeing with tepid water.

When the buds break, rub out the weakest one, leaving only one on each side-shoot base. These buds should grow on into lateral shoots or fruiting spurs, on each of which a bunch of grapes should set. As soon as you can recognise the starting of the bunch of fruit to set, pinch out the shoot at the second leaf past the bunch. During this time the rod or leading shoot will be growing and making new side-shoots which should be shortened as already described in the work for the first year. Side-shoots from the rod can be tied to the supporting wire framework with raffia or fillis string. Should bleeding of the wounds result from pruning, cover the cut surfaces either with a vine styptic, seal with a red-hot iron or cover with a layer of sealing wax.

When the vine starts into growth in the spring, an annual top dressing of a mixture of well-rotted manure, peat and loam is all that is required, with bone meal replacing the manure if that is unavailable. During the summer months keep the vents open and a good circulation of air as much as possible, but at the first sign of mildew on the leaves spray with thiram or other suitable fungicide to control.

If the vine is planted inside the greenhouse, watering is extremely important, always giving sufficient to soak the soil thoroughly. Remember, too, that no roots can take in fertiliser unless it is completely soluble, and therefore the quantity and the quality of the crop you are expecting must obviously depend a great deal on the watering and feeding you give it.

At the end of the growing season – August or early September – less ventilation should be given so that the warm sun will ripen the fruit. Also remove any surplus shoots which may be shading the grapes from the sun. To make sure that you are quite *au fait* with this pruning business, may I just make it clear that when the main rod has reached the top of the greenhouse it should be pruned each year, and the lateral shoots on the main rod cut back to one or two eyes (buds) during the dormant period. See that the laterals or spurs are at least 1 ft apart, and you can allow some of them to grow on, when they should be trained horizontally and secured to the supporting wires. Always remember that the bunches of grapes are borne on the current year's shoots, and that will give you a clearer insight into the ideas behind vine pruning.

Pollinating the flowers is an important function essential to fruit production. When the vine comes into flower, the atmosphere of the greenhouse should be kept somewhat drier than before. Syringeing should cease for a time, at least until the fruit has set. It is not always necessary to resort to artificial pollination, but it is advisable in most cases to assist the process either by gently passing a soft camel-hair paint brush or a rabbit's tail over the flowers, or by shaking the vine stem about noon each day to distribute the pollen. Within a few days of pollination the grapes will set, and afterwards increase fairly rapidly in size. Now is the time to keep the greenhouse warm and moist.

The 'thinning' of the bunches and berries is most important, because it is by this that we systematically direct the flow of sap to produce grapes of good size and quality. It should be done about a fortnight or so after the fruitlets have begun to form, when they are about the size of sweet pea seeds. It is much better to start the thinning early than to leave the job until the fruits are nearly full size. For this job a pair of long-pointed grape scissors is used, together with a small forked stick with which to steady the bunch when working.

First, cut out the small unfertilised grapes and any that are discoloured or malformed. Next thin out those in the centre of the bunch so that all the young grapes are left at least ½ in. apart, giving them sufficient space to grow and expand. Whilst there is no tap to control the flow of sap to a bunch of grapes, it is obvious that an amount of sap being distributed amongst, say, thirty grapes will produce much better fruit than the same amount of sap being shared between, say, fifty grapes. This is, of course, the reason for thinning.

A few weeks after the grapes have set, they may appear for a time to have stopped swelling. Don't be unduly alarmed – the reason is that they have reached the stoning stage, and for a short time the temperature may be allowed to fall slightly. After a matter of almost days when the swelling of the fruits restarts, increase the temperature and humidity to normal.

Those who grow grapes in an unheated yet sunny greenhouse must take a little extra care to get them to ripen. When the grapes are colouring the greenhouse should be ventilated freely during warm weather in the daytime, but the vents should be closed in the afternoon to compensate for the lack of artificial warmth. The air inside the greenhouse must be kept as dry as possible after the grapes have begun to change colour.

The bunches should be cut when they are fully mature, and handled with extreme care. Some gardeners cut the bunches from the rod with a portion of the stem attached and insert the end of the stem into a bottle filled with water. In this way they will keep for much longer.

The vine may be propagated by five different methods – seeds, cuttings, eyes, layering or grafting. The best and most popular method is by striking 'eyes' or buds in heat in February. From a pruned shoot cut off a 2 in. length with a plump but dormant bud in the centre. With a sharp knife slice a strip of wood from the underneath of the cutting on the opposite side to the bud. The prepared 'eye' or bud is then pressed (bud uppermost) into a pot containing a mixture of equal parts of coarse sand and peat, with the tip of the 'eye' remaining above the surface. Place the pot on a propagating case where a bottom heat of 21 °C (70 °F) is produced, and keep moist. Once rooted, the bud grows quickly, and may be ready for planting out by early summer.

Vine cuttings about 1 ft long can be rooted in the autumn, but as a rule they seem to give less satisfactory results than the single 'eye'.

My two favourite varieties are 'Black Hamburgh' (the old favourite but still one of the best) for a cold greenhouse and 'Madresfield Court' for a heated one. They both produce delicious large bunches of black grapes.

The most troublesome pest of the vine is the vine weevil, the grubs feeding upon the roots and the adult weevils on the leaves – but we'll talk about that in the next chapter.

Powdery mildew and downy mildew are two diseases to watch out for, both really the result of too much warm humidity with poor air circulation. Treatment may include Bordeaux Mixture, Lime Sulphur, Dinocap, Thiram etc., but again this is a subject for Chapter 15.

15 Pests and diseases

Permanently and completely disease and pest-free plants in the greenhouse may be a pipe dream, but at the same time this must be the ultimate aim of all keen greenhouse gardeners. Even pests and disease must play their part in the natural cycle of things, but a greenhouse automatically creates artificial environments and situations which must therefore be approached and then treated scientifically if sometimes unnaturally. Hence the tremendous upsurge in the popularity and usage of the new, and even systemic, fungicides and insecticides. No longer can we rely upon the good offices of the ladybirds, the centipedes etc. to keep down what seems to be a greater population of pests than ever before, and somehow we seem to be losing the art (or is it craft?) of building up a plant's health and strength to resist disease by giving it ideal cultural conditions under which to grow.

As in a nursing home, high levels of greenhouse hygiene can be of primary importance in keeping pests and diseases at bay, and we talked about this in an earlier chapter. Cleanliness, of course, is one of the main factors in the subject of hygiene, and at least once a year (usually autumn) the greenhouse glass, timber, metal, as well as all pots, pans, etc. should be thoroughly washed with a disinfectant solution. (Jeyes' Fluid is still as good as any!).

It pays to keep a regular and constant eye on each individual plant in the greenhouse to ensure that they are in good condition and show no signs of attacks by pests and/or diseases.

There is ample proof that a healthy plant is capable of resisting many of the troubles which ordinarily attack weak plants. Plants in poor condition often allow diseases and pests to take hold, and it is for this reason that I would advocate the discarding of any plant not in good health.

Rubbish should be kept from accumulating beneath the greenhouse staging or in odd corners, as this could provide a breeding place for many pests. Another thing, of course, is that, like humans, pests can actually be the means of carrying disease spores from one plant to another.

Besides pests and diseases, upsets and troubles can be caused to plants by 'disorders'. As they are usually the result of poor cultivation, bad drainage, wrong temperatures, draughts, unacceptable degrees of humidity or dryness etc., these disorders can usually be treated without resorting to chemicals – in fact, just readjusting the conditions to suit the plants.

But let's start with PESTS, and get to know our enemies . . . .

Pests

Aphides

Usually called *Aphis*, this is a large family of 'suckers' which includes greenfly, white fly and black fly, and which is probably more numerous in your garden than any other type of pest. Practically all plants, wild or cultivated, act as hosts to one or more kinds of aphis. They feed by sucking the sap from the tissues of the plants, and have an extraordinary rate of self-propagation. Actually, each individual aphis does not produce an abnormally large number of young, but the offspring commence to reproduce soon after birth. When you think that a greenfly born today could be a grandmother in ten days' time, it makes you realise that if wasn't for the up-to-date methods of aphis-extermination we should be knee-deep in them before you next prune the roses.

Aphis eggs are laid in autumn and hatch the following spring, giving rise to wingless females which, shortly afterwards and without apparent male intervention, produce living young for about three weeks. Long before this period is over many of the young will themselves be engaged in similar rapid reproduction. At the end of the season a generation of true sexual aphides appears, and these lay the eggs which over-winter on the host plant and hatch the following spring. They primarily cause damage by sucking the sap of plants and so weakening them, often to the extent of causing their

One of the problems of spraying is that it is so often done only on the top leaves, whereas the pests are on the undersides of the leaves or safely tucked away in the centre of the plant. Fairly forceful sprays should be applied to the plant from all angles, but be careful not to hold the spray nozzle too near to the actual plant or the concentration and force of the liquid insecticide may damage tender tips. Remember you are trying to spray the aphides not blow them off! One other aftermath of greenfly attack is that they excrete a sticky honeydew on which sometimes there develops a fungus known as 'sooty mould'. (Get rid of the aphides first, then treat the sooty mould with lime sulphur or Bordeaux Mixture.) The presence of greenfly also encourages ants, which feed on the honeydew and seem to fuss over and tend a colony of greenfly as a farmer and his staff would care for a valuable herd of dairy cows. Therefore the ants must also be destroyed, and a ready means of getting rid of them is to dust their runs and suspected nesting places with one of the several proprietary ant powders or liquids. Ants are more likely to be present where the soil becomes very dry under the staging, so that occasional sprays of water there will do good.

death. Some kinds of aphis cause malformations such as curling leaves or even swellings or galls of various forms.

Fortunately there are very many methods of reducing the aphis population, the most effective being the newer systemic insecticides. These actually enter the system of the plant through the roots or leaves and poison the sap, so that the next nibble the greenfly has is his last! Unfortunately, most of these systemic insecticides may not be used on chrysanthemums, asters, salvias, begonias, nasturtiums, zinnias and most pot plants, so their uses in the greenhouse are very restricted. However, there are quite a number of safe contact insecticides, either with a derris or pyrethrum base, but for control of green or white fly I find that Malathion is the most effective. (Hydrangeas, crassulas and dahlias are allergic to pyrethrum.)

The horrible little white fly is a persistent fellow and difficult to eradicate. It will attack many pot plants, but one of its most popular hosts is the cineraria, so do have the Malathion ready to use as soon as you see the whites of their eyes. Fumigation of the whole greenhouse with 'smoke bombs' is perhaps an even better means of dealing with these awful pests. There are many so-called 'smoke bombs' on the market, which, if used rightly, will effectively clear most pests from the greenhouse without harming the plants in any way. The manufacturers' directions should be read very carefully, however, as there are certain plants which are allergic to fumigants.

Chrysanthemum midge

This had been a serious pest in America for some time before it was first discovered here. Damage can be recognised by malformation of shoots and buds, on which small but conspicuous gall-like swellings containing eggs are noticeable. BHC sprays are effective in mild attacks, but in severe infestations the best policy is to burn the affected plants.

Earwigs

These do more damage outside than in, but they are particularly fond of and do great damage to the flowers of chrysanthemums. They are nocturnal feeders, but sprinklings of BHC dust or periodic use of sprays based on BHC usually afford ample protection from this pest. In fact a greenhouse earwig hunt with a powerful torch after dark often provides a successful bag.

Eelworm

These microscopic true worms, belonging to the group known as nematodes or thread worms, are among the more serious causes of injury to plants. Few pests

Plate 85 Male earwig on flower. Earwigs feed on the
petals of various flowers, causing clean-cut holes

increase more rapidly, and the great number of types of eelworm which exist means that they attack a wide range of plants. Each species seems only able to attack a certain range of plants, hence the phlox eelworm, the bulb eelworm, the potato eelworm etc. Sometimes they cause gall formation, as in the case of the root knot eelworm of tomatoes, and, of course, they also attack chrysanthemums. Eelworms may live within the tissues or on the surface of plants, and their presence can often be detected by washing the affected tissues in a little water in a watch-glass and examining them with a hand lens.

The life history of the majority of eelworms consists of the laying of tiny, oval, transparent eggs which hatch and give rise to offspring resembling their parents. These young worms rapidly grow to full size and that's when the trouble begins.

Apart from the heat treatment of plants by means of root immersion into hot water and certain doubtful spraying methods, few true remedial measures are known. In the greenhouse, of course, soil may be freed of eelworms by means of steam sterilisation, but as treatment of individual plants is so difficult it is usually much safer for the amateur to uproot and burn the whole plant before others are attacked. The remaining soil in the pot could then be steam sterilised or treated with Formaldehyde.

Plate 86   Mealy bugs on pelargonium

Leaf miner

This is a tiny grub or maggot that tunnels its way within the tissue of a leaf, leaving irregular wriggly light-coloured channellings showing clearly and distinctly. If the attack is severe, remove the leaves and burn them, but if you catch it early you may even be able to discern the grub channelling away at the end of the line. Pinch it out and there is one less leaf miner to worry about. To control this pest, which mainly attacks chrysanthemums and cinerarias in the greenhouse, spray with Lindex or any BHC insecticide, and repeat the treatment two or three times at weekly intervals. You could also fumigate with a greenhouse smoke such as Marfume Lindane, based on BHC (BHC by the way, stands for benzene-hexachloride, a very important chemical base for many proprietary insecticides). Where cinerarias are concerned, 'smokes' are preferable during autumn and winter when moisture should be kept off the foliage.

Malathion is also an effective spray against leaf miner.

Mealy bug

This is a tiny bug-like creature with an oval-shaped body, somewhat flattened, and covered with a white mealy wax. They breed all the year round under glass, laying tiny groups of eggs in a surround of woolly material. They attack many kinds of plants, and are amongst the most difficult of all pests to dislodge. If they are found on plants like cacti or succulents, try to rub them off with a soft cloth soaked in a mild insecticide, or even pick them off with a pointed stick of soft wood. Mealy bugs also shelter in crevices of the bark of grape vines and suck the sap. If this is the case, apply methylated spirit to the rods, with a stiff paint brush when the vine is dormant in the winter. A BHC 'smoke' could also be used – but not when the vine is in bloom.

Red spider mite

Related to the true spider which, incidentally, can be the gardener's friend, the red spider mite is a serious greenhouse pest. The damage caused by these horrible little villains is due to them biting the leaves of the plants, usually on the undersides, and then sucking the sap. The leaves then generally turn mottled yellow or greyish-white and may, later on, die and fall prematurely. The whole plant could succumb to a vigorous and sustained mite attack. The red spider mite is a minute creature

about $\frac{1}{16}$ in. in length – to the naked eye a mere dot of rust. The winter is spent in the adult mite condition, the colour being brick red, and it hibernates in cracks, pots, soil, woodwork, in fact wherever it can find shelter in the greenhouse. I mention this so that you can formulate your own battle plan, spraying, disinfecting etc. Under glass the mites become active during March or April and eggs are laid. The young mites have only three pairs of legs, but soon cast their skins and produce four pairs as in the case of the true spider. The length of life is about twelve days, but a large number of generations is produced during the season. It is encouraged by hot, dry conditions, and its presence is often noted by

greyish leaf markings. Remember that red spider mite cannot thrive in a humid atmosphere.

Treatment is more or less as for aphides, with pyrethrum, derris and Malathion all effective at certain stages of the mite's life cycle. Fumigation is of course most important, remembering that azobenzene smoke generators can actually destroy the eggs of red spider on plants. This should then be used to the makers' instructions in April or May.

Scale insects

This is really a group of insects which actually includes mealy bugs. It also includes the following greenhouse trouble-makers:

The Soft Scale. Not easy to detect owing to the fact

Fig. 19   Thrips – adult and larva

that their colour tones with that of the plant on which they are feeding.

The Camellia Scale. Favourite host plants include begonias, camellias, asparagus fern and figs.

The Orchid Scale. Attacks many kinds of orchids and palms.

The Aspidistra Scale. Aspidistras, of course.

Viewing the group as a whole, the female scales may be recognised by their immobility on the plant or by their waxy coverings. The males sport a single pair of wings, are often waxy and usually red or yellow in colour. They have no mouths and therefore do not feed, but the females make up for it by sucking the sap from the tissues of the plant.

Eggs are laid usually in a waxen sac, made by the female, which hatch into young which are tiny, flat and oval in shape, and can walk. The larvae grow and pupate and males may emerge, although those which turn to females gradually lose their legs and form a scale over their bodies.

From tender-foliaged plants individual scales can be removed with a small camel-hair paint brush or pointed soft wooden skewer, and infected leaves can be gently sponged with dilute washes of derris, Malathion, or pyrethrum.

Routine fumigations of the greenhouse with BHC or nicotine 'smokes' will destroy the scale insects but not their eggs, and except for plants with tender foliage, thorough spraying with one of the above insecticides is recommended.

Thrips

These minute insect pests, black or dark yellowish-brown and about $\frac{1}{16}$ in. in length, attack a wide range of plants, including chrysanthemums, carnations, strepto-carpus, gloxinias, begonias and many foliage plants. Leaves, stems and flowers become mottled or streaked and distorted, and carnation flowers show distinct white flecks when attacked by thrips. They are an absolute menace, but let's look at the life cycle of this quick-propagating pest, which seems to revel in hot, dry greenhouse conditions.

Their winter is spent in the soil in the partly-grown larva stage, from which they emerge in the spring to complete their growth and become adult.

Thrips lay small kidney-shaped eggs in slits in the leaves or stems of plants, the slits being made by their short blade-like ovipositors. The young thrips which hatch from the eggs are pale yellowish-brown in colour, very tiny and without wings. The skin is cast a number of times. With successive 'moults' the wings gradually form, and finally the perfect winged adults appear.

Besides the direct injuries produced by the laceration and sucking of the tissues of plants, thrips are now realised to be instrumental in spreading certain virus diseases of plants as, for instance, spotted wilt disease in tomatoes. As we said before, they must be carriers. To combat this menace, keep a degree of humidity in the greenhouse, fumigate with nicotine or BHC and spray with Malathion.

Vine weevil

This little horror not only attacks grape vines, but pot plants in the greenhouse and raspberries outside as well. As the conditions suit it better, it does far more damage inside than out of doors. The grubs feed upon the bulbs or roots of plants and the adult weevils on the leaves. They are very partial to hydrangeas, cyclamens and begonias. They have no wings, are about $\frac{1}{4}$ in. in length with a black body which is rough and pitted.

There is only one generation of the weevils each year, but they usually live for two seasons. They lay their eggs in groups of five to fifty in the soil in pots between February and October. Funnily enough, the eggs are usually laid in the pots whilst they are in the open or

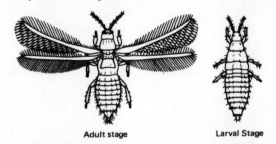

Adult stage   Larval Stage

in cold frames. (Perhaps the fresh air gives them the urge to lay!) The grubs which hatch are white in colour and legless, feeding on the underground portions of the plants – roots, bulbs, corms etc. The grubs are fully fed by the end of the autumn, and they then construct tiny cells in the soil in which they pass the winter. In the spring the grubs turn to pupae within their cells, and the weevils emerge in May.

Plants whose roots are being attacked by the grubs

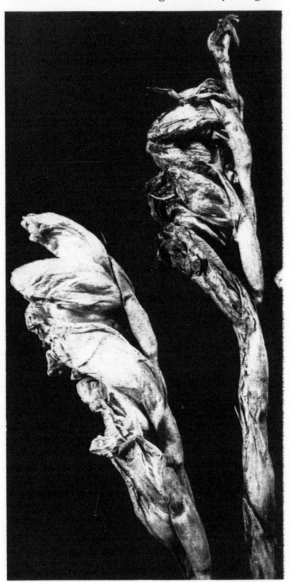

should be repotted in fresh soil to which Murphy's Sevin Dust (Carbaryl Insecticide – successor to the now banished DDT) has been added.

If you see sign in your greenhouse of nocturnal vine weevil activity – leaf margins nibbled etc. – then a Lindane smoke, set off last thing at night when the greenhouse is closed, will do the job and clear the adult pest.

Woodlice

These pests feed on a variety of different foods, including vegetable refuse. Living plants in the greenhouse may also be attacked when woodlice do a great deal of harm to the roots, leaves and even stems.

Woodlice form a section of the group known as Crustacea (which includes crabs and lobsters) and are not insects. They are about $\frac{1}{3}$ in. long and have seven pairs of legs.

They like dark, damp situations such as rotting woodwork etc., so first of all remove all likely nesting places. and then sprinkle BHC dust around the greenhouse,

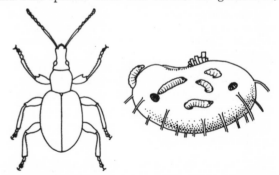

Hollowed-out potatoes or apples left overnight will trap woodlice, so that the following morning they may be removed by hand and destroyed.

So much for the main greenhouse pests, now let's have a look at some of the principle indoor plant DISEASES:

Diseases

Botrytis cinerea

This is a common fungus perhaps better known under the name of *grey mould*. (All diseases are caused and spread

Plate 88   Vine weevil. Nocturnal in habit, the adult feeds on foliage of fruit trees, shrubs, and ornamental plants under glass

Fig. 21   Woodlouse

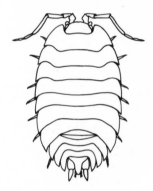

Damping off

This is the most serious trouble which can afflict seedlings of almost every kind of garden plant being raised in boxes or pots, causing them to turn brown, shrivel and collapse. The delicate seedling is easily infected by various fungi commonly present in soils, especially if the con-

ditions are too wet or too sour for the healthy growth of the plant.

Badly-infected seedlings should be taken out and burned, the soil being dumped outside, too, but if the attack is not too severe the disease can be checked by watering the soil and seedlings with Cheshunt Compound. This treatment is better used as a preventative on the soil before the seed is sown. Prevention lies in using only sterilised soil in pots or boxes which have been sterilised with a formalin solution, and seeing that the soil is not too wet or the conditions too humid. Thin sowing of the seeds and very careful watering will also reduce the likelihood of the disease appearing.

Downy mildew

Although the spores of this disease are visible as a 'mildew' on the surface of the leaves, the body of the fungus is inside the tissues, and therefore it is not a true mildew. It is, however, a fungus which attacks grape vines and which can be recognised by the small greenish-yellow spots on the leaves, with a delicate whitish mould on the underside. Later the spots become brown and cracked. Attacked fruits become quite useless – they get hard, turn greyish-blue in colour and finally brown and shrivelled.

by fungi spores, and sometimes the name refers to the disease and sometimes to the fungus.)

It thrives only where there is ample moisture, causing brown or grey fluffy growth on leaves etc., the affected tissues eventually turning black, soft and rotten. Slightly raised small spots surrounded by rings of pale green, on tomatoes, is also held to be due to infection by the spores of the grey mould fungus (this infection is some-times called *Water Spot*). Normally tomatoes affected by botrytis have a pale whitish look at the stalk end.

The best way to keep clear of this disease is to avoid the close, damp cool conditions in which it flourishes. Remove and burn all affected leaves, fruits and tissue, and pay close attention to ventilation and reduction of humidity. Strawberries, lettuces, melons, cucumbers and tomatoes are all particularly susceptible, so watch out for the trouble, remembering that prevention is better than cure. Spraying is not usually necessary although Orthocide will normally check the disease, but on edible crops it is safer to dust frequently with flowers of sulphur. (See Plate 16.)

The fungus likes warm, humid conditions, so keep a good air circulation in the greenhouse. At the first sign of the disease spray with a fungicide such as Dithane or Bordeaux Mixture.

Foot rot

This is a similar disease, but one which attacks older plants. Among the greenhouse subjects which are sometimes attacked by foot rot are tomatoes, calceolarias, carnations, pelargoniums, schizanthus and petunias. It cannot flourish where there is a good circulation of air, so that ventilation is important. See that soils are well drained and be careful with the watering, particularly when the plants are not in full growth between autumn and spring.

Foot rot describes the blackening and shrinking of the stems of plants at the base, and is caused by soil fungi. Young plants seem to be more susceptible at low temperatures. Here again, Cheshunt Compound applied with normal watering should keep foot rot in check.

Leaf spot

This is a fungus disease of chrysanthemums most prevalent in wet seasons. First signs are small brown spots on the leaves or brown areas on the margins. These quickly enlarge and may develop to affect the whole leaf. It usually starts on the lower foliage and spreads upwards if not checked. Dithane, Benomyl or Bordeaux Mixture will control.

Mildew

True mildews are fungi which grow over the surfaces of the plant, not inside the tissues as with botrytis. All mildews are parasitic, obtaining their nourishment by means of processes that penetrate the epidermal cells – the main body of the fungus is always entirely outside the plant.

The white, powdery appearance of the mildew is due to the formation in chains of large numbers of spores that spread the disease in the growing season. Later in the summer another kind of spore is produced inside small black fruit bodies, which protect the spores so that they can survive the winter and infect crops again in the spring. These black bodies can be seen, with the aid of a pocket lens, resting in the mildew.

Fortunately satisfactory control methods are available to control mildews. The fungus being exposed on the surface of the leaf makes it readily accessible to sprays. Most fungicides will kill mildews, especially Karathane, those based on sulphur, Benomyl, or Dithane, so it is not a bad idea to keep a puffer loaded with flowers of sulphur handy in the greenhouse. Karathane 'smokes' are, of course, very effective, too, but do keep a sharp lookout for signs of the white powdering on the leaves of plants in the greenhouse which will mean that mildew has struck again.

Rusts

This is the term applied to a group of microscopic fungi which are found all over the world, and are parasitic on all kinds of plants. There are different rusts peculiar to literally hundreds of different species of vegetable, fruit, foliage and flower, and most of them show up as small but clearly-defined reddish-brown spots on the undersides of leaves. On tomatoes rust shows up as yellowish blotches on the upper surfaces of the leaves, while beneath will be found a greyish mould, turning to a velvety-brown or purple. When severe, the leaves may become covered with the mould and shrivel up. Badly infected tomato foliage cannot be cured – it must be removed and burnt, after which the plant should be sprayed or dusted with a sulphur or thiram fungicide.

Again, too much moisture and poor air circulation can be contributory factors in causing an outbreak of rust, and again careful attention to cultivation and hygiene must be the order of the day.

Stem rot

Sometimes known as *stem canker*, this is a disease to tomatoes as well as geraniums, causing the shrinking of the stem at the base. It is not a common trouble, and when it occurs it is best to destroy early infected plants. Water any remaining plants not affected with Cheshunt Compound at the bases, and take steps to sterilise the soil for a future season.

Tomato blight

Although this disease is more troublesome to outdoor tomatoes (it also affects potatoes) there is always a possibility of it getting into the greenhouse. The symptoms are dark brown or purple patches on leaves and

Plate 89   Tomato leaf mould (*Cladosporium fulvum*).
Attacked foliage

stems with whitish edges of mould on the undersides of leaves. Infected fruits are blotched brown and soon begin to rot. Infected foliage should be removed and burned, but this disease is better prevented rather than cured. Prevention lies in covering the plant surfaces with a fine film of a copper fungicide, and avoiding conditions which are too damp and muggy.

Virus diseases

The spores of virus diseases are infectious and may be transmitted from disease to healthy plants by contact with the infected sap, but are mainly spread by biting and sucking insects which visit healthy plants after having fed on diseased ones. A virus disease in a plant is systemic and once present in the sap it passes to all parts, with the possible exception of the seed. There is no known cure, so infected plants must be burned as soon as any symptoms become apparent, before they are a source of infection to other healthy plants.

On tomatoes and cucumbers, *mosaic* is a common virus disease, with mottled light and dark green blotches showing on the leaves. If the attack is only mild, the

plants may be allowed to fruit, but if severe, it is best to burn them without delay.

Spotted wilt is also a serious virus disease which attacks the tomato causing brown spots on young leaves with arrested tip growth. Infected plants should be promptly destroyed. As this disease may be carried by such plants as gloxinia, dahlia, arum, solanum etc. it is unwise to grow greenhouse flowers with tomatoes.

On strawberries, *yellow-edge* is a virus disease which shows as a dwarfing of the youngest leaves with yellowing around the edges. This is usually most noticeable in the latter half of the season.

Crinkle is another virus disease of strawberries where the yellowing occurs in spots over the leaves as well as at the edges, and the leaves become wrinkled. Virus-infected strawberries should be removed from the greenhouse immediately and burned, as of course should any plants found to be infected by any virus disease. Sometimes foliage becomes distorted and malformed, but if there is any doubt it is better to be safe than sorry. After handling affected plants, make sure you wash your hands in a disinfectant solution.

So to sum up: the chief symptoms by which you may recognise various virus diseases are those of a mosaic or mottling of the leaves, or streaking and distortion, with malformation of the flowers and stunting of the plants. Greenhouse plants susceptible include chrysanthemums, begonias, calceolarias, cinerarias, lilies, primulas, zinnias, besides tomatoes and cucumbers.

Probably the ultimate solution to the virus problem lies in the breeding of virus-immune plants. In the meantime, however, control lies primarily in the planting of healthy virus-free stock, good cultivation and pest control, with the prompt destruction of infected plants.

Many different viruses can infect pelargoniums (geraniums) and plants may be infected with several at the same time.

Pelargonium leaf curl virus shows as yellow spots (sometimes star-shaped) on young leaves produced in the winter months. Because surrounding tissues continue to grow the leaves become crinkled, hence the name. *Pelargonium ringspot virus* appears as yellow or pale green rings, spots or line patterns on leaves produced during the summer months. This virus seems to affect ivy-leaves more than zonals. The warning here is to always make sure you purchase virus-free stock. *Bacterial leaf spot and stem rot* is often widespread in pelargoniums and can cause severe losses, infecting roots, stems and leaves. The first symptoms are minute translucent dots on the undersurface of leaves which enlarge, and are sharply defined as circular or irregular brown sunken spots. They then may enlarge further and appear on the upper leaf surface as round brownish spots, which in turn may increase in size to cover most of the leaf and cause the veins to dry out. Stem infections on mature plants first appear as wet areas which darken and turn brownish-black, spreading up and down the stem. Eventually the infected stem shrinks and turns completely black. Stem cuttings may be similarly infected, often caused by the bacteria being spread by contaminated knives, plant-to-plant contact or even infected potting compost. Both zonals and ivy-leaved geraniums are very susceptible to leaf spot and stem rot. Control measures apart from normal use of fungicides, consist of discarding and burning plants showing symptoms, avoiding wetting the leaves and stems, strict hygiene precautions and good insect control. Stand stock plants on slatted benches rather than sand, which can spread the disease through root contact and irrigation watering.

Functional Disorders

So far as functional disorders are concerned, here are a few which may affect your tomatoes:

Cracking and splitting of the fruits are traceable to either fluctuating supplies of sap, weather changes or too much direct hot sun. If watering is withheld for only a short period, the tomatoes tend to harden their skins as the consequent flow of sap is reduced. Then the watering is recommenced and the flush of sap exerts sufficient pressure to burst the skins and cracks or splits appear on the fruit. Constant and regular watering, mulching of the soil and shading from hot sunshine offer preventative remedies.

Blossom-end rot is clearly defined when the end of the tomato opposite the stalk has a round brown crinkled patch, later sinking and turning black. This is caused by the plant having suffered a serious water shortage at a critical stage in the fruit development. It is not, of course, infectious, and if more attention is given to watering will not occur on later ripening fruits.

Plate 90   Tomato splitting

Scald is a round whitish patch on tomatoes and is attributed to the effects of strong sun on fruits near the glass of the greenhouse. (Grapes may also be affected by scald.)

Green back, when the area round the stalk does not colour properly, is related to the shoulder of the fruit becoming too hot under strong direct sunshine, and possibly a shortage of potash. The remedy is to shade the tomatoes from hot sunshine, and see that the roots have enough potash.

Blotchy ripening is often due to lack of potash and unbalanced soil nutrition.

Dry set, when blossoms do not drop but the fruit remains tiny and undeveloped, is due to faulty pollination and a too-dry atmosphere. Mist-spraying of flower trusses when open will prevent this.

Functional disorders of chrysanthemums includes yellowing of the upper foliage which is a sign of stagnation at the roots and is usually due to overwatering. Yellowing of the lower leaves indicates dryness at the roots, or it may be a sign of starvation. Chilly winds early in the season may cause some leaves to turn a reddish tinge, but don't worry – like us in unseasonable weather – they

soon get back to normal.

I cannot end this chapter – or even this book – without putting forward the point of view of those who abhor

the use of toxic chemicals in the battle against pests and diseases. Whilst sincerely respecting their viewpoint and agreeing that the thoughtless and uncontrolled use of chemicals in the garden would be a dreadful mistake bringing ultimate disaster, I feel I must represent the majority of commercial growers and dedicated gardeners and say that in this modern day and high-speed age the

only acceptable approach to the control of pests and diseases must be the positive and direct. And that means using chemicals, the form of control which is always most successful. Unfortunately the chemicals used must be carefully studied and selected as some can have harmful effects on crops at certain stages of development. There is also the potential danger to man and the beneficial insects in the food chain.

A food chain is the name given to the complex feeding system in a natural community. Each link is eaten by the one above and any toxic chemicals present will thus be passed on to the top of the food chain.

For example, a possible community living in a garden

could consist of roses, aphides, ladybirds, blue tits – and above them a bird of prey such as the hawk. The aphides or greenfly feed on the sap of the roses, the ladybirds eat the greenfly and are in turn eaten by the blue tits, and these may then be killed and eaten by the hawk. Certain toxic chemical insecticides sprayed on to the roses to kill the greenfly will become concentrated in the creatures above and might also kill them. Thus the ladybird, the blue tit and the hawk could suffer from the effects of a chemical intended to kill greenfly only. (In fairness I must mention that there is at least one natural insecticide called pyrethrum which will not harm pets or birds.) Man belongs to similar food chains but fortunately, due to his enjoying a very varied diet, the chemicals rarely build up to a harmful level. Wild birds and insects are of course much more rigid and fixed in their diet, and are therefore more susceptible to the effects of the chemicals.

Perhaps I am painting this lurid picture of mass murder far too vividly. Many chemical insecticides, including DDT and Aldrin have already been banned because their ultimate and possible danger to the health of man was suspected and later accepted. Those have now been replaced by modern insecticides which have been fully tried, tested and proved to be incapable, under normal circumstances, of building up to a harmful and dangerous level. Nevertheless this aspect of chemical usage is under constant review by horticultural scientists.

Some growers, as a change from other methods, use biological methods of control. It is a well-known fact that ladybirds feed on greenfly and some growers, particularly in America, have experimented by rearing and distributing large numbers of ladybirds on to the crops to clear an attack of greenfly.

Similar control of red spider mites in the greenhouse is possible by releasing red spider mite predators on to the crops there. This can be an effective control for some infested crops, particularly the tomato.

This is all very well, and interesting to me because I love birds and hate to see their destruction, but we must be sensible and practical. Just think of the time and cost involved in breeding and restraining until required a sufficient number of predators to clear an attack of greenfly or red spider – and anyway, isn't this tantamount to a declaration of war? Even if only in the insect world, the principle involved is the same, so raise swords you greenfly and defend yourselves!

Index